Home *for* Christmas

Anita Stansfield

Covenant Communications, Inc.

Published by Covenant Communications, Inc.
American Fork, Utah

Printed in the United States of America
First Printing: October 1997

04 03 02 01 00 99 98 97   10 9 8 7 6 5 4 3 2 1

ISBN 1-57734-205-4

Chapter One

"What do you mean, you're not coming home for Christmas?" Michael Hamilton bellowed through the phone, his rich Australian brogue coming across the miles as clearly as if he were in the next room.

"Just hear me out, Dad." Allison attempted to explain. "It's just not going to work out. I really *want* to come home for Christmas . . . but I just can't."

"Why?" he pressed. "Give me one good reason."

"I could give you a lot of reasons. But the bottom line is simple. I've prayed about it, Dad." She had told herself over and over she was going to get through this phone call without getting emotional. But the tears refused to be held back. "I can't explain it, really. I just know I need to stay here for Christmas."

Michael sighed loudly. "Well, we certainly can't dispute the answer to prayers. But we'll miss you."

"I'll miss you, too," she said; then there was a long silence, broken only by Allison's occasional sniffle. She'd only had one Christmas at home since she'd returned from her mission. And while she was enjoying her classes at BYU, and she knew it was the right thing for her, she truly missed her home and family.

"Do you want me to have your mother call when she gets home, or—"

"I'd love to talk to her, but . . . will you tell her? Smooth it over for me, okay?"

"I'll do my best," he said.

"Hug all the kids for me." She sniffled again, imagining her little brothers and sisters and all she would miss by not being with them through the holidays.

"I will," Michael said. "You take care now. Call if you need anything—and I mean it!"

For several minutes after she hung up, Allison stared at the phone, as if it might somehow take away the discouragement she felt.

"Maybe you *should* go home for Christmas." Startled, Allison turned to see her roommate, Sariah Mitchell, fluffing her long, black hair with a towel. "I mean . . . you look pathetic, girl."

"It's that obvious, eh?" Allison scowled and fidgeted with the magnets on the refrigerator. "I just don't get it," she added. "I mean . . . I *know* I'm supposed to stay. But . . . *why?*"

"I guess it's a faith thing," Sariah suggested. "Maybe by the time Christmas gets here, you'll know."

"I'm sure you're right," Allison said as her thoughts drifted home all over again.

"Hey," Sariah nudged Allison, "I think you need to get out and do something besides work and study."

"Yeah, like what?" Allison scowled.

"My brothers are coming by in an hour to take me ice skating. Why don't you come along?"

Allison really didn't feel like going out. She couldn't remember the last time she'd gone ice skating, and she felt certain she wouldn't be very good at it. But she had to admit she needed a distraction from thinking about home. She hadn't been this homesick since the beginning of her mission.

"Come on," Sariah insisted. "It'll be good for you."

"Well," Allison admitted, "I certainly can't come up with a good excuse *not* to go."

"Good," Sariah beamed, and Allison went to her room to dig out her thermal underwear. In spite of being so far from home, she had to admit to being grateful for such a good friend.

In appearance, Allison and Sariah had nothing in common beyond their average height and build. Allison's pale, lightly freckled skin and strawberry-blonde hair were a stark contrast to Sariah's more exotic appearance—the result of a unique blend of ancestry. Allison and Sariah had met in a humanities class, and had quickly become good friends. *Spirit sisters*, they often said in reference to the closeness they shared. Allison had been immediately struck by Sariah's unique beauty. The mixture of races in her blood came through with soft features intensified by a smooth, dark complexion, dark eyes, and rich black hair. In spite of their differing backgrounds, they'd enjoyed sharing an apartment for the last three months, and had found that they were especially compatible.

While Allison was digging through her drawers to find a pair of gloves, Sariah called from her bedroom across the hall that her brothers would be there any minute. Sariah spoke often of her three big brothers, one of whom was newly married. The boys had teased her mercilessly as a child, but had become her protectors as they'd grown. Allison hadn't given much thought to what they might actually be like. She was surprised to come out of the bathroom and find three of the most adorable men she had ever seen, standing in the front room of the apartment, teasing Sariah about her striped hat and gloves.

"I think they're cute," she protested lightly. "You guys just don't have any taste, that's all."

Sariah turned to see Allison standing there. "Are you ready?" she asked. Allison nodded, trying not to gape while she pondered the idea that it just wasn't fair for one family to have so many gorgeous people. The brothers were all equally tall, with varying degrees of curl in their black hair. Their features differed enough that it might be difficult to recognize them as brothers, if not for their identical coloring. The dark complexion and eyes were downright compelling.

"This is Allison," Sariah said. "Try to behave in her presence, if that's possible." She chuckled softly and added, "Allison, meet my brothers: Ammon, Helaman, and Mosiah."

Allison couldn't resist expressing her first thought. "You guys aren't the three Nephites, are you?"

They laughed so hard that Allison was almost embarrassed.

"That's pretty good," Helaman said. "Why didn't we think of that years ago?"

"Actually," Mosiah added, "I think we're the three Lamanites."

"Well," Helaman chuckled, "we do have some Lamanite blood in there somewhere, don't we?"

4

"It's a pleasure to meet you, Allison." Ammon stepped forward and offered a hand. Allison reached out to accept his hearty handshake, reminded of the way a fellow missionary would have greeted her during her mission.

"And you," she said.

A moment later, a blonde woman came through the door, protesting dramatically about how cold it was outside. "Are you sure you want to go skating? It's freezing out there."

"That's what makes it fun," Mosiah said to the woman as he put an arm around her. It was easy for Allison to surmise that Mosiah was the married brother, and this was his wife.

"Oh," Sariah said as she zipped up her coat, "that's Sally. Sally, meet Allison."

"Hi," they both said at the same time, then they laughed.

"Well, shall we go?" Ammon asked. "The truck's running."

"Can we all fit in there?" Sariah asked with a wrinkle in her nose.

"Of course we can," he insisted.

Allison was relieved to see that the truck—a new Dodge—had an extended cab. Helaman, Sally, and Mosiah piled into the small backseat, where Sally sat mostly on her husband's lap. Allison and Sariah got in the front with Ammon, who was driving. He stuck a CD in the stereo that played *Charlie Brown* Christmas music, then Allison felt him gently nudge her leg.

"Sorry," he said as she realized he couldn't get to the stick shift unless she moved her legs.

"I should have sat in the middle," Sariah said.

"On the contrary," Ammon added as they pulled out of the parking lot. "Allison's a lot cuter than you are."

Allison passed off the compliment and tuned in to the laughter going on behind her as it became evident that Mosiah was tickling his wife. When she finally got him to stop, the brothers talked and laughed about things that made no difference to Allison. But she still enjoyed the way their happiness rubbed off on her.

At the rink, Allison felt ridiculously unsteady on the ice. Sariah prodded her along until she could move forward without feeling too shaky, then they went together once around the rink. Allison paused at the edge to catch her breath while Sariah looked skyward and made a comment about what a beautiful night it was, in spite of the cold. And a moment later, Helaman erupted out of nowhere and took hold of Sariah's arm. "Come along, little sister," he said, skating away with her.

Allison smiled as she watched them sail off. She wondered what it might be like to have a big brother. Allison's two half brothers were so much younger that it was difficult to imagine them as adults. She looked toward the sky and attempted to suppress a sudden yearning for home.

"Hey," Ammon startled her as he came to an abrupt halt at her side, "what are you doing over here by yourself?"

"Just enjoying the scenery," she insisted.

Without her permission, Ammon took Allison's hand and led her into the flow of skaters gliding around the rink.

"I'm really not very good at this," she protested.

"You're still standing," he grinned endearingly, and Allison realized they were gaining speed. As if he sensed

6

her sudden nervousness, Ammon slipped an arm around her waist, and within a minute they were skating in perfect unison. "See?" he smiled. "You're practically a pro."

"Only because you're practically holding me up," she said with a little laugh, unable to deny that she was enjoying herself.

"What were you thinking back there?" he asked. She looked disoriented and he added, "You seemed a million miles away."

Allison marveled at his perception as she answered. "I guess I was—several thousand miles, at least. I was thinking about my brothers."

"And where are they?"

"Home . . . in Australia."

"Ah," he smiled, which made him all the more adorable. "I thought I detected a bit of an accent. Although you certainly don't sound Australian; at least not like the Australians I've heard."

"Actually, I was born here in Utah, and lived here until I was nearly ten. After my father died, my mother married an Australian and we moved there. I guess it's rubbed off on me some through the years."

"Well, it's rubbed off very nicely," he said.

Allison wondered if he was always this sweet. While she found him every bit as attractive as his siblings, she was preoccupied with a certain wistfulness at not having a big brother. She'd experienced such a relationship somewhat with Sean O'Hara, a young man her parents had taken in. He'd practically become a part of the family, but it just wasn't the same. At the moment, with Ammon beside her, she felt so . . . what? Secure? Protected?

"So, how old are your brothers?" he asked.

"Ten and fourteen," she answered.

"And do you have others in your family, or—"

"I have three sisters. I'm the oldest."

"Sariah tells me you're not going to make it home for Christmas. That must be tough."

Allison nodded, not wanting to talk about it. She continued to skate in Ammon's care while he rambled comfortably about his own family. Allison enjoyed hearing some of the same stories she'd heard from Sariah, told from a different perspective.

Finally, Allison declared that her legs needed a rest. "I'm pretty out of shape," she said, moving carefully to a bench where Sally was adjusting the laces on one of her skates. A quick glance told her that Sariah and Helaman were still out there, laughing together as they did simple little spins in the center of the rink. It was obvious the family had done a lot of ice skating. Allison shared some small talk with Sally, then Mosiah appeared with two cups of hot chocolate.

"Here," he said, handing one of them to Allison.

"Oh, I don't need to take your—"

"It's for you," he insisted. "Ammon's getting more." He sat by Sally and whispered something that made her giggle. Allison closed her eyes and inhaled the steam that rose from her cup. A minute later, Ammon appeared with two more cups, handing one to his brother.

After a long break, Allison skated some more with Sariah, feeling a lot more confident after skating with Ammon. They talked and laughed as they circled the rink. Then Ammon spent some time skating with his sister, while Helaman escorted Allison around for a while. He was every bit as charming as his brother. She wondered about their birth order, and their different personalities.

When they couldn't take the cold any longer, the group piled into the truck again. This time, Sariah and Allison sat in the back with Helaman in between them. Allison noticed Mosiah putting an arm around his wife and briefly kissing her. A twinge of loneliness caught her off guard.

Allison's main goal at this point in her life was not by any means to catch a husband. She was enjoying her education and her job, and knew there were plenty of years ahead for marriage and children. But the failed relationships—three since her mission—had made her wonder if she'd ever find anyone she could really settle down with and be happy.

She found it difficult to sleep that night as her mind wandered to thoughts of home, conjuring up clear images of her family gathering for the Christmas celebrations. Her thoughts merged into dreams as she finally drifted off to sleep. She was with her mother, wrapping garlands around the stair railings and weaving pine boughs into wreaths that would hang on every door. She was with her brothers and sisters, trimming the tree and rolling cookies. It all seemed so real that she could almost smell the pine and taste the buttery dough.

A bell ringing in the distance pulled her into consciousness. Allison sighed as she absorbed the morning sun pouring through the apartment window. She wasn't home at all. "Please, dear Father," she prayed aloud, "if I'm supposed to stay here, give me something to make it worthwhile. I'm trying to have faith, but—"

A loud knock at the door startled her. As she hurried down the hall to answer it, trying to get into her bathrobe at the same time, she realized the ringing that had awakened her was the doorbell. She pulled open the door and momentarily caught her breath. It took her a moment to remember which of Sariah's brothers this was. "Ammon," she said, hoping she had it right. She was still half asleep.

"I'm sorry. Did I wake you?"

"It's okay. I need to get going anyway. I've got to be at work in an hour or so."

"Is Sariah—"

"Oh, she got a call late last night. She's filling in at work for somebody who got sick."

"Oh, I see," he said, his disappointment obvious.

Through an awkward moment of silence, Allison self-consciously realized that she'd just gotten out of bed and she probably looked horrible. But Ammon gave her a genuine smile, saying, "You have a good day now."

He started to walk away and she asked, "Do you want me to tell Sariah anything, or—"

"No, it's not important," he insisted. "I'll talk to her later."

Allison closed the door and leaned against it, feeling better for some reason. She reminded herself to have some faith. Surely the Lord had *something* in mind for her this Christmas. She just had to put it in his hands and hope for the best.

Chapter Two

Allison had barely taken a step away from the door when the bell rang again. She pulled it open to see that Ammon had come back.

"Hey," he said, "if you can't go home for Christmas, maybe you should spend it with us."

Allison's eyes widened. "Us?"

"Sariah . . . and, well . . . all of us. We're having Christmas with my grandmother this year. She lives on a farm out in Spanish Fork. My parents are flying in from Oregon. Since all of us kids are out here, they figured that would be easier. And, well . . . there's nothing like Christmas with Nana."

Allison was stunned. She knew well who he was referring to. Sariah had talked endlessly about *Nana*, her mother's mother. Her real name was Guadalupe—or Lupe, as she preferred to be called. Lupe was a full-blooded Mexican who had married a Native American at the age of seventeen. Lupe's husband of forty-seven years had passed away four years earlier, and her life now revolved around her children and grandchildren. She had several spread across the country, all of whom she kept closely in touch with through long letters. She was especially close to Sariah and her brothers. In fact, Mosiah and Sally were currently living in Lupe's basement while they were going to BYU. Lupe had been born and raised a Catholic, and she lived her religion vehemently, in spite of many attempts by her Mormon grandchildren to convert her.

It only took a moment for Allison to conclude that Christmas with Nana certainly had appeal, but she was caught so off guard that she didn't know what to say.

After a moment of awkward silence, Ammon said, "Well, it's just an idea. Think about it."

"Thank you," she managed. "I'll talk to Sariah, and . . ."

He smiled and waved, walking away once again. And again, Allison closed the door and leaned against it. Was this the answer to her prayers?

That evening, after Sariah and Allison had both returned from work, Allison mentioned Ammon's visit. "Did you tell him to invite me to spend Christmas with your family?" she asked pointedly.

Sariah's innocent expression answered the question immediately. Then she broke into a broad grin. "No, but that's a fabulous idea! I'm ashamed that I didn't think of it myself. Well, I probably would have . . . eventually. But . . . oh, you *have* to. It would be great!"

While Sariah French-braided Allison's hair, she talked on and on about Lupe, who kept her Mexican culture alive through her extraordinary cooking and holiday traditions. Sariah talked about her love of Lupe's culture, and the unique way she blended it with the Native American background of her grandfather. She also spoke of the other side of her family. Her father's father was half African-American; he had married a Polynesian woman who introduced him to Mormonism. Sariah's parents had smoothed their unique mixture of ethnic backgrounds together with a strong conviction as Latter-day Saints. Her mother's family had migrated to Utah because of work opportunities. It was there that Lupe's second daughter, Maria, had met Paul Mitchell, who had swept her off her feet and baptized her—all in the same month. Paul and Maria had a strong commitment to the gospel; therefore, the Church was elemental in Sariah's upbringing. She and her three brothers had all gone on missions, and from what Sariah had told her, they were all as strong in their testimonies as she was.

The two young women switched places, and while Allison French-braided Sariah's hair they talked more about the prospective Christmas celebration. Allison had to admit that she felt better already at the possibility of being included.

"Are you sure it's all right if you bring a tagalong?" Allison asked as she twisted an elastic around the bottom of Sariah's braid.

"Of course," Sariah laughed. "Nana always says that the fuller the house, the happier the people in it. She'll be delighted."

When the braids were completed, they went out for chili-cheese fries and a movie, enjoying the time together since they'd each had a relationship turn out badly not so long ago.

"Actually," Sariah said on the way home, "I must admit that I'm glad you're staying for Christmas. It might be selfish of me, but I'd miss you if you left."

13

Allison had to admit she felt a little better. It was nice to be blessed with a good friend.

Allison's mother, Emily, called the next day, and Allison was glad to be able to tell her about her holiday plans with Sariah's family. Emily admitted she would miss her daughter dreadfully, but it helped to know that she wouldn't be alone for Christmas.

The first week of December, Allison bought gifts for her family. Sariah helped her box them up, and they were shipped to Australia with plenty of time to arrive before Christmas. Sending the package off triggered a fresh spell of discouragement. Again, she questioned her reasons for not going home, wondering if it was only her imagination that had made her believe staying in Utah was the right thing to do. She truly enjoyed her job, doing accounting for a major department store, and she was determined to make it on her own and take care of herself. She felt certain that taking time off to go to Australia would jeopardize her job, but she wondered if it meant enough to her to compensate for missing Christmas with her family. She had to remind herself that her job was only part of her reason for staying. She just knew it was right to stay. That's all there was to it.

For a few days, Allison thought of little besides Christmas at home. Her memories of the holidays were always warm and bright. Of course, having her mother marry a man who was independently wealthy had been an obvious blessing to the family. But the very fact that Christmas had always been nice, yet conservative, exemplified the lifestyle Michael provided for them. The magic of Christmas for Allison had not been in the abundance of gifts and goodies, but in the spirit that filled

14

their home as preparations were made with the true meaning of Christmas emphasized every step of the way.

Allison's only dark memories associated with Christmas were from a time of rebellion prior to her mission. It was still difficult for her to understand why she had made some wrong turns and distanced herself from her family. Those Christmases away from home were something she'd rather not think about; but perhaps they were the very reason she treasured being with her family so much now.

Steering her mind back to the good years of her life, Allison thought about going by horseback to cut a tree and bring it down from the mountains that bordered their land. She thought about the party they always had for her father's employees, many of whom had no family. At first, Allison's thoughts only heightened her dismay about not being a part of the celebrations this year. But as she prayed and thought it through more carefully, the generosity and gratitude she had grown up with remained with her—in spite of the miles separating her from home.

Attempting to keep her thoughts in Utah, Allison became preoccupied with Sariah's family. She wondered why she found them so fascinating. Perhaps it was the diversity of cultures that made them so unique . . . and yet their standards and beliefs made them much like the other Mormons she knew. She pondered the possibility that seeing all the siblings as adults, enjoying each other and spending time together, was difficult to comprehend, since her own siblings were all so much younger. Whatever it was, she was grateful for the opportunity to be a part of their family at this time—even if it was to such a small degree.

Allison was excited when Sariah invited her to have dinner at Lupe's home on Friday evening. The family was doing a Christmas project, and Sariah had said it would be a chance for her to get to know the family a little better before Christmas. She explained their family tradition, which Lupe and her husband had begun the first year they'd come to Utah. They would each bring donations of toys and non-perishable food and goodies, then put together some packages to leave anonymously with families who were struggling.

Allison looked forward to it all week, and was dismayed to realize she would have to work late on Friday. Sariah insisted that she come anyway, so Allison hurried to get everything done and lock up the office. A light snow was falling when she started the drive to Spanish Fork, trying to remember Sariah's directions. She almost got lost a couple of times as she explored the back roads in the dark. She was about to give up and go home when she noticed Ammon's truck sitting conspicuously in front of a large farmhouse, situated back off the road in a cluster of huge trees.

Allison trudged through the snow and stomped her feet as she rang the bell. She could hear laughter on the other side just before the door flew open and Helaman exclaimed, "It's about time you got here! Now we can have some fun." He took the bag of things she'd brought to donate to the project, and she was pulled into a whirlwind of activities that didn't leave her even a moment to think about home.

Allison was first introduced to Lupe, who was not at all what she had expected. She was a refined, stylish woman who wore her gray hair in a tightly-wound bun at the back of her head. She took Allison's face into her tiny hands, saying with enthusiasm, "Oh, you sweet thing. I've heard so much about you. I'm so glad we get to have you for Christmas!" Her voice had a subtle accent that added a layer of charm to her demeanor.

"*You're* so sweet to let me come," Allison countered. Lupe hugged her tightly with a merry little laugh, and Allison noted that she smelled of pressed face powder and a subtle aroma of roses.

Lupe heated up a plate of supper for Allison; enchiladas unlike anything she'd ever eaten before. She found it difficult to believe that Mexican food could taste so good. It had never been one of her favorites, but she knew now that she'd never tasted *real* Mexican food.

Lupe then took Allison on a tour of the big, old farmhouse. Mingled with a variety of Christmas decor was an abundance of knickknacks and memorabilia sitting about, and the walls were covered with pictures. But everything seemed to have some significance, and the house felt spacious and clutter-free, as if each item was in its proper place. Lupe told Allison the stories behind several objects and pictures, making it clear that this woman had committed her life to her family and her Christian beliefs. It didn't take much to realize that in spite of her determination to remain aloof from Mormonism, Lupe lived her life according to the Bible. Scattered throughout the home was evidence of this as well, with little statues, ornaments, and pictures that represented her beliefs.

Lupe talked about her keepsakes and pictures with an occasional catch in her voice as it became evident how much she missed her departed husband. She spoke of his Native American culture with great admiration, and the decor in her home emphasized her love of it, delicately combined with her appreciation for her own Mexican upbringing.

In the upstairs hall, Allison admired Lupe's wedding portrait, while Lupe recalled the day in amazing detail.

"You're monopolizing her, Nana," Ammon said, startling them both. They looked over to see him leaning against the wall, watching them.

"Oh, if Allison wants to—" Lupe began in an apologetic tone.

"I can assure you I'm thoroughly enjoying myself," Allison insisted. "Lupe can monopolize me any time she wants." Ammon smiled at this and Lupe laughed softly as she exchanged a warm glance with her grandson.

"We're about ready to go deliver these things," Ammon said. "I assume you want to do the final inspection."

"I certainly do," Lupe said. Then to Allison, "We must find time to visit again soon."

"I'll look forward to it," Allison said, and followed them down the stairs.

Allison was amazed to see half a dozen large wicker baskets, decorated with big red bows and filled artistically with a variety of offerings, sitting on the front room floor.

"We did it from your lists," Sariah said, "but if you want to adjust them, then—"

"They look beautiful, as always," Lupe exclaimed. "The addresses are on the list. You know what to do now."

Helaman glanced over the list in his hands and asked, "How do you come up with people who need these every year, Nana?"

"God has a way of providing such things," she said matter-of-factly.

Allison had been a part of many charitable projects in her youth. Michael Hamilton was a generous man who made many opportunities to share his wealth anonymously. But as everyone but Lupe piled into Ammon's truck, much as they had on their ice-skating excursion, Allison couldn't recall ever having so much fun.

While Ammon drove, he began a histrionic speech, mimicking *Mission Impossible*. The others laughed as he rambled, ". . . Your mission, Mr. Mitchell, is to deliver these goods unnoticed. Those who have been assigned to assist you are varying in expertise, and—"

"Give it up," Helaman interjected after he'd gone on for several minutes.

Allison marveled at the way Sariah's family behaved like a group of mature children. By the time they delivered the sixth basket, they had the routine down to a science. After parking the truck up the street in the shadows, they all slipped out, giggling softly. They moved quietly toward the appointed home, ducking behind cars and trees in a manner that was completely ridiculous. While the appointed pair hurried to the porch, knocked and ran, the others waited behind parked cars, attempting to observe the receiver's reaction. Allison had trouble keeping her laughter silent as she saw the way Sariah's brothers ran and dove into their hiding places like a combat team in a war movie.

They returned to Lupe's house and gathered around the huge table in her dining room to play *Uno* until Lupe served hot cocoa and homemade pie. Sariah insisted she had to leave to get some homework done, but they talked Allison into staying.

The gathering around the table eventually dispersed somewhat, but Allison remained in her chair while Helaman told her a couple of funny stories about his childhood memories in Lupe's house. When he'd finished, she gathered up a few dirty dishes and took them into the kitchen. She hesitated when she saw Lupe talking quietly with Ammon. She couldn't hear what they were saying, but it was evident that Lupe had been crying by the way Ammon gently wiped the tears from his grandmother's cheeks, then he hugged her close to him and she laughed softly. Allison was about to turn around and discreetly leave, but Ammon glanced over and saw her.

"I'm sorry," she said. "I didn't mean to intrude or—"

"Oh, don't think a thing of it," Lupe insisted, apparently not embarrassed. "I'm just a silly old woman who can't stop missing my sweet *viejo*." (Sariah told Allison later that she wasn't certain exactly what the word meant, but it was the term of endearment Lupe had always used for her husband.)

"Christmas just isn't the same without him," Lupe added.

"I think that's understandable," Allison said, setting the dishes in the sink.

"He was a grumpy old coot, and you know it," Ammon said with a teasing smile.

Allison was a little surprised at the comment, but Lupe laughed and slugged him playfully in the shoulder. "I know. That's why I miss him."

Allison insisted on helping Lupe wash up the dessert dishes while the three Nephites cleaned up the dining room, and Sally dried dishes and put them away. When it seemed that everyone was leaving, Allison thanked Lupe and trudged back out to her car. The bright spirit she'd felt through the evening came crashing down when the motor wouldn't start. She was still sitting there, hopelessly grinding the ignition, when the door flew open and startled her.

"I don't think that's going to help much," Ammon said. "Come on. I'll give you a ride home."

"But . . . I need my car tomorrow, and—"

"Well, if it won't start, it won't start," he insisted, and what could she do but agree?

On the ride home, while Allison was preoccupied with wondering how she was going to get to work the next day, Ammon and Helaman sat on either side of her, talking between themselves. It was easy to surmise that Ammon was a contractor, and Helaman was a pre-med student. Ammon told his brother over the top of Allison's head how some job had fallen through, and he was grateful he'd learned a long time ago to save money through the abundant months in this business in order to get him through the lean times. He said he would be fine for several weeks, and some other job was scheduled to begin soon after the new year. He believed it would be a good one. Allison realized then that Helaman worked some for his brother, which supplemented the income he got working as a waiter. Allison wanted to ask which restaurant Helaman worked at, just so she could go there to eat and admire him. But she was too preoccupied with her incapacitated car.

"Hey, stop worrying." Ammon nudged her with his elbow.

"What makes you think I'm worrying?" she snarled, albeit lightly.

"Maybe it's the way you look like you could bite somebody," Helaman interjected.

"Why would I be worrying?" she asked with sarcasm. "My car is stranded in Spanish Fork, and I have to get to work. I'm sure that Sariah can give me a ride tomorrow, but what about—"

"Helaman's not too bad with cars," Ammon said. "I bet you could talk him into some cheap mechanic help. If he gets ornery with you, I could at least tow it for you tomorrow. And hey, I'm out of a job at the moment. I don't live so far away. I'm available as a cheap chauffeur."

Allison had to admit that the prospect of having some help made her feel better already. "How cheap?" she asked.

"Oh, he's *cheap*," Helaman said, then Ammon scowled at him and Helaman laughed.

Allison tried not to think about her car as she attempted to sleep that night. Sariah had said that taking her to work wouldn't be a problem, and Helaman had told her he was going to help Lupe with something tomorrow and would take a look at the car while he was there. Allison finally forced her mind back to earlier in the evening, recalling the enjoyable time she'd had with Sariah's family. She drifted to sleep with the image in her mind of Ammon Mitchell tenderly wiping away his grandmother's tears. *What a wonderful family*, she thought, then silently thanked her Father in Heaven for allowing her the opportunity to be a part of their lives while her own family was so far away.

Chapter Three

Allison was awakened abruptly by a ringing phone. She grabbed for it, and heard Sariah say hello from the extension at the same time she did.

"Could I speak to Allison?" a woman's voice said.

"This is she," Allison said, and Sariah hung up the other phone.

"Allison, this is your aunt, Louise. I'm calling from Arizona. I doubt you'd remember me, but—"

"You're David's wife," Allison said, attempting to be coherent. She couldn't remember the face, but she knew the name from her grandmother's letters.

"That's right." Louise sounded pleased. "I know you've kept in touch with your grandmother through the years. I found your number in her address book, and—"

"What's happened?" Allison interrupted, her heartbeat quickening.

"Well, you know of course," Louise sounded calm and gentle, "that your grandmother's health hasn't been good for quite some time, but . . . well, she's had a mild stroke, Allison. Along with that, it seems that her other struggles have weakened her considerably, and . . . well, the doctors tell us she hasn't got much time. I knew you were the only one in your family who's in the States right now, and . . . I just thought you should know."

Allison asked Louise a few questions, then told her that she'd keep in touch.

While Sariah was driving Allison to work, she briefly explained the situation.

"So, this is your blood father's mother," Sariah clarified.

"That's right. And . . . well, we've kept in touch, but . . . the truth is, she's a difficult woman to like. My sisters are too young to even remember our father, so they've not had any relationship with her. And Grandma never liked my mother much, for reasons I'll never understand."

"Well, are you going to go see her, or—"

"I don't know how I possibly could," Allison insisted. "I could never get the time off work without jeopardizing my job. I wonder if she's capable of talking on the phone. Maybe I could just call her."

Sariah said nothing more, but Allison sensed that she was surprised by Allison's attitude. After work, Allison called her mother to talk it over.

"Do you think I should go see her?" she asked Emily right off.

"I suppose that's up to you, sweetie. You're the one who has stayed close to her through the years."

"Well, we've exchanged letters, but I wouldn't say we're close."

"You're the only one who can decide what's best, Allison," Emily said gently. "If you decide to go, we'd be happy to cover the airfare. Just let us know."

Allison hung up feeling a little disgruntled. Perhaps she'd been hoping that her mother would assure her there was no logical reason to make the trip to Arizona. In any event, she wasn't entirely happy about having the decision left on her shoulders. She reminded herself that she was entitled to her own personal revelation, so she prayed about it that evening, then attempted to sleep. While she was weighing her options, straining to come up with every possible reason *not* to go to Arizona, Allison had a clear image appear in her mind of Ammon Mitchell tenderly wiping his grandmother's tears. Of course, *his* grandmother was sweet and lovable and filled her life with caring for her posterity. Joan Hall, on the other hand, was belligerent and harsh. Then she recalled the question she'd often asked herself when difficult choices came up. *What would Jesus do?*

Allison called first thing the next morning to make arrangements for a flight to Arizona. She was even able to get a budget fare that she could afford to pay for on her own. She found it interesting that once she made the decision, all the confusion and guilt fled. She knew she was doing the right thing. Her boss wasn't very happy about her taking the time off, but her aunt Louise was thrilled to hear that she would be coming.

Sariah took Allison to the airport, and Louise picked her up when she landed in Arizona. The change in climate was a pleasant surprise. During the hour-long drive to the house, Louise chattered about the family and the circumstances of her grandmother's health. She asked Allison questions about her own family and showed genuine interest.

"I'll never forget how shocked we were at your father's death," Louise said gently. "He was such a good man."

Allison was surprised, after all these years, how the comment made her tense, even vaguely upset. Was it because of the pain she'd felt over losing her father, or the knowledge of her father's faults that made it difficult to hear him described as *such a good man*? Not knowing what to say, she just listened as Louise went on.

"I always thought so much of your mother, as well. I wished we hadn't lived so far apart; I think we could have been good friends."

"She's said the same about you," Allison said, and Louise smiled.

"Anyway, after your father died, we just lost touch. I know she had her differences with Joan. I think Joan somehow wanted to blame your mother for losing her son."

Allison absorbed this revelation and wondered if it might be true. She'd taken more than one psychology class, and truly enjoyed what she'd learned. But she'd never thought to use it in analyzing her own family.

As Louise continued to talk, Allison marveled at what a good woman she was. She had taken the ornery Joan Hall into her home and cared for her for many years, because the other members of the family were not willing to do it. Even as she explained this, she managed to avoid saying anything critical or negative. Louise spoke of her love for her husband and children, and Allison began to get an image in her mind of what kind of family Louise had. When they arrived at the house, her expectations were dashed.

David and Louise's oldest child was married and living a few hours away. The next was on a mission. There were three left at home, the youngest being thirteen.

Allison met her cousins graciously, seeing some resemblance to her sisters. It was more difficult than she'd expected to see her uncle David again. She'd not seen him since her childhood, and his resemblance to her father was almost eerie. His thinning hair had touches of gray, and she tried to imagine what her father might look like now, had he lived.

As Allison ate with the family and continued to observe them, she began to see Louise's sweet demeanor in a new light. The children were subtly rude with her, and she apparently expected little, if any, effort out of them in the home. It didn't take long to see that the children followed their father's example. His indifference toward his wife, and his subtle put-downs, bristled Allison's nerves. How could she not remember her father's less-than-kind treatment of her mother? She'd learned that behaviors were often the result of family cycles, and the evidence in this family was all too apparent.

While Allison helped Louise clean up the kitchen, her teenage cousins watched television with their father. Then Louise drove Allison to the hospital to see her grandmother. David showed no interest in going, saying he needed to read the paper. The children shared his lack of enthusiasm. Allison wanted to shout at them, "Don't you know she's dying, for heaven's sake?" But she bit her tongue and found it a relief to get out of the house and be alone with Louise. As they drove, she pondered the reality that Louise was sweet and meek—to a fault. She doubted that Heavenly Father expected his daughters to be so kind that they were treated badly. Then she recalled that this was a concept her mother had taught

27

her—after Emily had learned not to allow her own husband to be unkind and unfair.

The reality of seeing her grandmother was more difficult for Allison than she'd expected. They'd not seen each other for a long time, but they had exchanged many photographs. Joan Hall's health had obviously deteriorated a great deal. She'd aged years in a matter of months.

"Go ahead and talk to her," Louise whispered. "It's difficult for her to speak, but she can understand you."

Allison took hold of her grandmother's hand and looked into her eyes. "Grandma?" she said, leaning closer. The aroma of pressed face powder brought back memories of Joan's visits when she was younger. Allison also recalled the same scent hovering around Sariah's grandmother. It was obviously something common for that generation, but Allison found it intriguing that a dying woman would want to have her makeup on.

"It's Allison," she said when the old woman only looked confused. "Do you remember me? It's been so long."

Joan's eyes showed recognition, and something close to a smile touched her expression. She mumbled something that Allison couldn't understand, but Louise seemed well practiced at listening to her. She easily interpreted, saying, "She's telling you that you've grown up very beautifully." Joan muttered something else and Louise added, "She's asking about your sisters."

Allison started talking about all the things they were doing. With Louise's help, Allison answered questions about her schooling and her mission, and Joan was obviously pleased with the visit. Allison was feeling good about the experience until Joan apparently became agitated and mumbled something in an angry tone. Louise looked hesitant to interpret, but all that Allison caught were the words *that woman*.

"It's okay, I'd like to know," Allison said quietly to Louise. Then she wondered if she should have asked as Louise repeated Joan's apparent disgust with Allison's mother. She criticized Emily's relationship with her son, and expressed her aversion to Emily's marriage to a foreigner, taking her grandchildren so far away. Allison quietly listened to Louise's meek interpretations and observed Joan's rising agitation.

Finally Allison leaned closer over her grandmother, taking her hand once again. "Grandma, listen to me," she said in a voice that was firm but kind. "I know that you and Mother never saw eye to eye, and that's okay. But you didn't know my mother well enough to understand what was happening." She leaned a little closer. "My mother is a good woman who always tried to do what she thought was best. I'm certain that when you were raising your family, you did what you thought was best. We all have our faults and imperfections, but judging another is not going to take away any amount of heartache. If you can't find peaceful feelings toward my mother before you leave this life, Grandma, I pray that you can understand the full perspective once you pass through the veil. Life is too brief and precious to waste it away with bitter thoughts."

As Allison absorbed her grandmother's stunned expression, she wondered where that little speech had come from. Thinking through what she'd said, it gave her a whole new understanding concerning her grandmother. There was no question that the Spirit had guided her, but she hadn't heard herself speaking so boldly by its prompting since her mission.

Joan Hall then turned with difficulty to look away, indicating by her expression that she had nothing more to say to Allison. Louise looked alarmed and concerned as she said, "I'm certain she's tired. Perhaps we should go."

Allison hesitated, not wanting to leave with ill feelings. She took a deep breath and pressed a kiss to her grandmother's face. "I love you, Grandma," she said, and they slipped from the room.

Allison wondered if Louise might say something about the conversation once they were alone. But she made no mention of it, as if it were simply not something she wanted to talk about. When Allison asked, "Do you think I was too harsh?", Louise simply said, "I'm certain you said what you felt you had to."

Allison felt frustrated. While she certainly wouldn't expect Louise to take sides, she was beginning to feel like the woman didn't dare form her own opinion about anything.

Allison slept little that night. She lay awake in the spare bedroom, pondering her conversation with her grandmother and the impact of this woman's attitude on her family. She wondered what her own family might be like if her father had lived. Would Emily be as meek and mousy as Louise? Would Emily's children have followed their father's example in mistreating their mother? Allison felt disconcerted to wonder if she, herself, might have had different attitudes if her life had continued on as it had in her childhood. The thought was unnerving.

Allison prayed and meditated, coming to the conclusion that it was good for her to have said the things she did. And she felt a little better when she returned to the hospital the next morning after breakfast.

Allison uttered a silent prayer as she entered her grandmother's room. Knowing this was likely the last time she would ever see her alive, she wanted their time together to go well—for both of them. She wondered if Joan was asleep, but as she sat carefully in a chair near the bed, the older woman's eyes came languidly open.

"Allison," Joan murmured, "you came back. Bless your heart."

Allison took her hand, feeling emotion rising. Already she felt her prayers had been heard. For some reason, Joan's speech, though a bit slurred, was much easier to understand today. If they could converse without Louise interpreting, it would be much easier.

"How are you feeling today, Grandma?" she asked gently.

"Oh, I'm just so tired," Joan said.

"Do you want me to let you rest, or—"

"Oh, no," Joan insisted in a strained voice. "Come closer, please. Let's talk."

Allison sat on the edge of the bed, continuing to hold her grandmother's hand. Louise smiled and touched Allison's shoulder, saying, "I'll leave the two of you alone for a few minutes."

Allison felt briefly nervous to be left alone with a dying woman, but Joan's eager expression soon calmed her.

"There's something I want to tell you," Joan said. "But I was never very good at putting words together, even before I had trouble talking." She smiled as if she'd made a joke, and Allison laughed softly in response.

"I'm listening," Allison urged gently.

31

"You know, my dear, I love all my grandchildren. And maybe it's not right to admit to having favorites. But you always had a special place in my heart. Even before your father died, there was something about you that was just so sweet . . . so much like your mother."

Allison's eyes widened. Was she being presumptuous to assume that Joan had just given her mother a compliment? Not knowing what to say, she just waited for her grandmother to continue.

"You know, of course, it was very difficult for me when your father died. But somehow I always felt like you understood my feelings, and perhaps you shared them. I'm certain I didn't handle losing him very well. Maybe I've always been a little crusty, but . . ."

Allison's chest tightened with emotion as huge tears welled into the old woman's eyes. "What is it, Grandma?"

"I want you to tell your mother that I'm sorry for the grief I might have caused her." Joan's hand tightened around Allison's, as if to emphasize her plea. "Tell her that I know she's a good woman."

"I will, Grandma. I promise."

Joan closed her eyes in apparent relief, and the tears spilled down her wrinkled face. Allison grabbed a tissue and wiped her cheeks. Joan chuckled with embarrassment, saying, "Oh, you're so sweet."

"Is there anything I can do for you, Grandma? Anything at all?"

"No," Joan smiled. "There's nothing anyone can do now. I'm dying, you know." For a full minute she became too emotional to talk.

While she was attempting to gain composure, Allison asked, "Are you frightened?"

Joan managed to nod, and Allison silently asked for some divine guidance in giving this woman the comfort she needed. Just as yesterday, the words came to her mind and she spoke them freely.

"You know, Grandma, the Lord understands your heart. He knows your weaknesses, but he also knows your strengths. He understands your struggles, and he knows that you have a good heart. It's never too late to make amends. I'm certain that when you leave this life, you will find great joy."

Joan nodded, but she didn't seem convinced. Allison felt compelled to add, "Just imagine your husband waiting there for you. The two of you were married in the temple. I'm certain he will be there. The two of you have been apart a long time. Why, I barely remember him."

A subtle peace rose in Joan's eyes, and Allison squeezed her hand. "I'm sure you're right," Joan said, and a minute later she drifted into sleep. Allison sat there, conscious of her grandmother's shallow breathing, until Louise came quietly back in the room.

"We should probably go soon, or you'll miss your flight."

Allison nodded and suddenly felt hard-pressed to keep from crying. She leaned over her grandmother and kissed her brow, whispering, "I love you, Grandma."

During the flight home, Allison contemplated her encounters with her grandmother. She felt they'd made some progress, but she couldn't help feeling some heartache on her behalf that was difficult to define.

Allison was glad to be going back to Utah. Not only had the visit been difficult, but she was beginning to feel the symptoms of a cold. Her head hurt, and her throat was a little raw and scratchy. She took some vitamin C that Louise had offered her, and had some orange juice on the plane. But she longed for her own bed and some good rest.

While Allison's thoughts hovered with her grandmother, she began to wonder what kind of difficulty there might have been in Joan's upbringing that she had passed on to her own children. The cycle of such things was too overwhelming to comprehend. It left her feeling somehow discouraged with the enormity of life's struggles. Certain that some time with her family would help, she wished she could go home.

As the plane landed in Salt Lake City, the pilot reported that it was snowing. Allison looked out the plane window and sighed as it taxied toward the gate. All this snow was just one more reason to want to go home. It was summer in Australia, and she missed it.

She gathered her things and hurried off the plane, anxious to share her feelings with Sariah. In spite of everything, she had to admit her gratitude for a good friend who would listen to her problems, care for her unconditionally, and give her some sound feedback. She passed through the gate door, took a few steps, and stopped dead in her tracks. Before her was a bright pink poster board with *Allison* written on it, punctuated with a huge question mark. Holding the sign was Ammon Mitchell, comically gazing past her, as if he had no idea who he was looking for.

"Is this supposed to be funny?" she asked, attempting to sound agitated, but a little laugh erupted by its own will.

Ammon showed exaggerated enlightenment. "Oh, you must be Allison," he said. Then he smirked. She laughed again and he added, "Apparently it's funny."

"I must admit it is," she said. Then more quietly, "Now put that sign away. You're embarrassing me."

Ammon comically put it behind his back, and she laughed again at the absurdity of his hiding something so huge and brightly colored. "Where's Sariah?" she asked, wondering if she was in the ladies' room or something. Perhaps Ammon had given her a ride because of the storm.

"She's home in bed," he stated. "She got some nasty flu bug that hit right after you left."

"Is she all right?" Allison questioned with concern.

"Oh, she's past the worst of it, I think. She just feels like she's been hit by a truck. Should we get your luggage and go?"

"This is it," she stated, indicating the overnight bag on her shoulder. Without her permission, Ammon took it from her to carry it.

"So, how was the trip?" he asked as they began to walk briskly through the long airport corridors.

"It was . . . interesting."

"That good, huh?"

"Yeah," she said with subtle sarcasm.

"Want to talk about it?" he asked.

Allison really didn't want to talk to *him* about it. She wanted to hurry home and talk to Sariah. But she attempted a brief explanation that would satisfy his curiosity, or at least return his politeness. By the time they got to the truck, Allison was surprised to realize she'd told him a great deal. He put her bag into the backseat and held her arm as she climbed in. As they pulled out of the parking garage and were assaulted with heavy snow, he commented lightly, "Maybe it's good Sariah couldn't come to get you. I'm not sure her little heap would make it through this weather over the Point of the Mountain."

"You're probably right," she replied, fastening her seat belt.

"So," Ammon said as they started onto the freeway, "do you think the trip was worth it?"

Allison thought about it. "Yes, I do. I'm glad I got to see her again. And I think maybe I left an impression on her."

"What do you mean?" he asked. Allison wondered if she wanted to tell him, but his manner made it easy to talk and feel comfortable. She repeated their conversations, and without really thinking about it, she rambled on about her feelings concerning the family and the situation. When Allison could think of nothing more to say, she expected Ammon to reply with some kind of blanket statement that would have been an appropriate response to discussing heavy issues with someone you were barely acquainted with. She was surprised, following a lengthy silence, to hear him say with fervency, "You know, I can't imagine trying to understand such things without the gospel. Isn't it wonderful to have the knowledge we have?"

"What do you mean?" she asked, intrigued by his approach.

Ammon went into a detailed explanation of his beliefs concerning the plan of salvation and how it applied to personal struggles, family dysfunctions, emotional illnesses, and other difficulties faced by mortals. He talked of this life being an extension of our previous existence, and how every human being was at a different level of progression. He elaborated on the beauty of life after death, and the possibility of the wrongs of abuse and other difficulties having new perspective on the other side. As Allison listened to him, the words she had said to her grandmother—words that had seemed to come from out of nowhere—came back to her, and they began to make sense. Of course, she had heard the principles he was talking about—many times, in fact. But she'd never been able to apply them in a way that seemed so logical.

The conversation filtered into a contemplative silence as they approached Utah Valley. It was snowing heavily, but Allison hardly noticed. Ammon seemed calm and confident. She became aware of Christmas music playing on the stereo and suddenly felt enveloped by an intangible warmth. She absently rubbed her arms as it heightened into an undeniable tingling.

"Something wrong?" Ammon asked.

"No," she smiled, "I think I feel better. Thank you."

"Hey," he said, "it's what Christmas is all about."

"What do you mean?" she asked once again, intrigued by his roundabout approach in conversation.

"Imperfections and struggles. The Atonement makes it possible to overcome them. As I see it, what we celebrate at Christmas is not so much the fact that Christ was born, as that he lived. And because he lived, and died, and lived again, anything is possible."

Allison took a deep, sustaining breath and contemplated that thought through the remainder of the drive. When they arrived at the apartment, Ammon helped her step down from the truck, then he carried her bag inside.

"Hey, thanks for the ride," she said. "I really appreciate it."

"I enjoyed it," Ammon said warmly.

"Can I reimburse you for the gas or—"

"Heavens, no," he laughed, then he slipped past her and knocked on Sariah's bedroom door. "Are you living, sis?" he called.

"Barely," she called back. Allison went to her room to unpack, aware of Ammon teasing his sister across the hall. She joined them for a few minutes to see how Sariah was doing.

"Do you need anything?" Allison asked.

"Oh, I'll take care of her," Ammon insisted. "You look like you could use a little rest yourself."

Allison was momentarily caught off guard. But she had to admit, "Actually, I wonder if I'm not coming down with something myself."

"I probably gave it to you," Sariah said.

"Not to worry," Ammon smirked playfully. "I'll take care of you, too."

Allison gave him a skeptical glance and went to bed. Within hours, the virus had taken hold with a harsh grip. Allison was amazed at how intensely her body ached, which was still not as painful as her head. She found some hope in the fact that Sariah was up and around, feeling better. And since she'd had exactly the same symptoms, she figured it was logical to expect the same time frame for her illness.

While Allison languished in her bed for seemingly endless hours, her mind wandered through the visit with her father's family. And the things Ammon had said about it. She was freshly amazed at his insight, but she still found her thoughts disturbing. It was difficult not to wonder how her own family might have been had her father lived. Of course, she believed that her mother would have continued to grow and improve in spite of her husband's struggles.

Thoughts of her mother spurred a fresh longing for home, and Allison turned her face into the pillow and cried. It seemed the harder she tried to convince herself she could be independent and make it on her own, the more she missed her family.

Chapter Four

Allison became vaguely aware of male voices and realized that at least one of Sariah's brothers was in the other room. A short while later, Sariah peered in and said, "I called in sick for you. Your boss didn't sound very happy, but I'm sure he'll get over it."

"Yeah," Allison replied with sarcasm, "or he'll get over *me*."

"I'm going to work now," Sariah added. "Do you need anything?"

"No," Allison lied, "I'll be fine."

"She's lying," Ammon's voice bellowed from the hall. Allison lifted her head, feeling guilt rush into her face. Then she groaned from the effort and lay back down, deciding she didn't really care if they thought she was a liar.

"She's miserable and lonely, but you have to go work. So go ahead, and *I'll* take care of her."

"What?" Allison lifted her head again, more quickly this time, and immediately regretted it.

"I said I would take care of you," Ammon said. Allison could hear Sariah chuckling as she left the apartment.

Allison wanted to yell at her and insist that she not leave her to deal with *a man* in this condition. But again the misery overruled, and she sank into the pillow. When it came right down to it, she was indifferent to anything but her aching head and body.

"Are you hungry?" he asked. She attempted to ignore him, but he repeated it.

"I don't know," she said. "I can't tell."

Allison's next clear awareness was of Ammon Mitchell standing above her with a cookie sheet that was apparently intended to serve as a bed tray. She managed to sit up, and he set it on her lap.

"Chicken soup," he declared, "fresh from the can. Nobody can do it like me."

Allison surveyed the tray, complete with juice, crackers, a napkin, and a silk rose that she recognized as being from one of Sariah's arrangements in the front room.

"Thank you," she said, then she stared at it for a minute, trying to get up the motivation to eat.

"Don't you want it?" he asked.

"It smells good," she said, realizing she *was* hungry.

"Then what's wrong?"

"I'm just tired."

"Do you want me to feed you?" he asked, and she was appalled to note that he was serious.

"I'm not *that* sick," she insisted. He smiled and she added, "Why don't you go . . . wash some dishes or something?"

"Okay," he said and left the room.

Allison had to admit she felt a little better after eating something. She took the tray to the kitchen, since she had to get up and use the bathroom anyway.

"Thank you," she said to Ammon, who had his head buried in the fridge. "It really tasted good. You're right—no one does canned soup like you do."

He chuckled. "You need anything else?"

"Just some drugs and some sleep." She took a dose of her cold medicine, went to the bathroom, and went back to bed.

Allison woke up with no sense of time. She found a note on her bedside table with her car keys.

There's more soup and juice in the fridge. Take it easy. Helaman got your car fixed. When you're up to driving, it's parked just outside your door. Ammon.

Allison sighed and laid back down. She had to admit she was being watched out for. "Thank you, Lord," she murmured aloud and drifted back to sleep.

The following day Allison felt no better, and talking to her mother on the phone didn't help any. It was good to talk to Emily, and it passed some time. But when she hung up, she felt even more alone. Sariah had left early and wouldn't return until late evening. She tried to study, knowing that finals were quickly approaching, but her head ached so badly she could hardly hold her eyes open.

Allison finally drifted to sleep on the couch late morning, with the thought that at least in sleep she could be oblivious. The phone startled her awake, and if she wasn't in a foul mood when she answered it, she certainly was when she hung up. A minute later, Ammon Mitchell knocked on the door, then stuck his head in and hollered, "Is anybody home?"

"Go away!" she snarled from the couch, pulling a blanket over her head. "I'm sick. I'm ugly. I'm fed up with life. And I don't want a man hanging around my apartment."

Ammon closed the door and leaned against it. "Don't beat around the bush, Allison," he said. "Be more assertive. If you have something to say to me, just say it."

As hard as Allison tried, she couldn't keep from snickering.

"I heard that!" he chuckled.

She peered up over the edge of the blanket and said, "Being outspoken hasn't been a problem for me since I was ten."

"Really?" he said with mock enlightenment. "I never would have guessed."

"What are you doing here, anyway?" she demanded. "Sariah won't be home until—"

"I'm well aware of my sister's schedule. I came to see if you need anything."

"Don't you have a life, Mitchell?"

"At the moment, no. That will change once I start work again after the holidays. Right now, I'm floundering in search of someone who needs some petty assistance and companionship. You're the best I could come up with."

"Oh, thanks," she said with sarcasm.

"Well, I hadn't even offered my help before you were kicking me out."

Allison sighed and stuck her chin above the covers. She had to admit it was good to know someone in the United States was thinking about her. "Sorry," she said. "I'm not having a good day."

"Is that the *fed-up-with-life* part?" he asked.

"I think so. I admit I've been having a hard time with not being able to go home for Christmas."

"That's understandable, but . . . well, maybe you should go." Then he chuckled and added, "I guess a ticket to Australia isn't cheap."

"No, but . . . well, that's not a problem, really."

"So, what else is bothering you?" he asked. She hesitated and he leaned forward. "If I'm being too nosy and you really want me to go, I'll just—"

"No," she said, "actually it's nice to have some company. I just got a call from my boss. He fired me."

"Can he do that?"

"I'm afraid he can."

Ammon sat down across the room and leaned back in the chair as if he had all the time in the world. He asked her questions and she talked. At first it was her mixed feelings about losing the job. She liked the work, but she had trouble with some of the people. "I guess I just want to know I can make it on my own," she said.

"I don't understand," he said. "It appears to me that you're making it just fine."

"I'm doing pretty good, actually. I guess it's something I need to prove to myself. You see, my father is—"

"I thought your father died when you were nine."

"He did. I mean . . . well, he's my stepfather, but he's much more than that."

"I understand."

"Anyway, he's independently wealthy." Allison hesitated after she realized what she'd said. She couldn't count the people who had changed toward her once they'd realized this one fact.

Without so much as a flicker of an eye, Ammon said, "And?"

"Well . . . he's a good man, and he's conservative. He

45

has a good attitude about the money, and he's taught me well. It's just that a lot of people don't seem to share our views, and I want to make it on my own. I want to get through college without leaning on my parents."

"Is it so wrong to get support from those who care about you, as long as you're working hard to improve your life?"

Allison couldn't answer that. She'd never thought about it quite that way before. When she said nothing, he went on, "So what have *these people* said that made you so determined to be self-sufficient? Not that I'm against being self-sufficient. I think it's great. I'm just . . . curious."

Just like the evening Ammon had driven her home from the airport, Allison found herself talking freely to him, as if she'd known him for years. She told him that although she wouldn't admit it to her parents, one of the biggest reasons she felt determined to make it on her own had stemmed from the hurt she'd felt after the third male interest in her life had changed toward her once he'd learned of her father's wealth.

Allison told Ammon the story of how Michael Hamilton had dated her mother in college for several months before she had any idea he was a wealthy man, then he'd come back into her life following her first husband's death. Michael was very quiet about his money. Allison respected his attitude about it, and she had followed his example of appreciating security while putting the emphasis of life on relationships and the gospel. But Allison had found that many people had trouble viewing her financial connections with such a healthy attitude. She had dated Mark for about two months before she casually mentioned something about her family that indicated their financial circumstances. After that, Mark had become almost phony with her, as if she lived some kind of a charmed life, and he was practically in awe of her.

She told Ammon how she had moved beyond Mark to a weekly date with a law student who was smart, witty, and not bad looking. She enjoyed their time together, until the wealth issue came up and he basically severed the relationship with a cryptic explanation that Allison interpreted as his feeling that wealth was wicked, and he wanted nothing to do with it.

"And then there was Joseph," she went on. "He was a pretty decent guy who actually came from a well-off family in South Carolina. I enjoyed our dates, and we had a lot in common. He treated me pretty well, and I became quite fond of him—more than any other guy I'd ever known. We actually talked some about marriage, and I seriously considered that he might be the one. But I began to feel uneasy when he came up with an occasional comment that made it sound as if our marriage would be some great merger of wealth and prosperity. He wanted our children to attend the finest private schools, and he would see to it that they enjoyed the best of everything. When I expressed my views about raising children to appreciate what they had, and to earn the things they acquired, the discussion became so heated that I knew this was not a man I could spend eternity with."

Allison went on to explain that in the weeks since Joseph had gone his own way, she had pondered the situation deeply. Was money such an important factor in relationships? She had been raised with the attitude that it was something needed to survive in the world, but it was the least important aspect of what life was all about. She believed that prosperity was a blessing to be appreciated and used wisely. She had seen countless examples of money being used to care for the needy and to make the world a better place, rather than being spent on acquiring material possessions.

"It baffles me," she said. "These are people who have supposedly been raised reading the same Book of Mormon that I've been reading. I mean, there isn't more than one version, is there?" Ammon laughed and she continued. "How can people of the same faith not see and understand the cycle that's taught over and over in that book? I just don't get it. How can Mormons have such differing views on money; views that come between relationships?"

Allison continued to ramble about her reasons for wanting to make it on her own and take money out of the dating issue. She had been trying to concentrate on her job and her education—both of which she thoroughly enjoyed, and which kept her mind off the painful evidence that good men were hard to come by. She mentioned that her mother had often advised her to enjoy life and not get caught up in worrying over it. "But," she finished, "I must not be doing something right, because I'm not feeling real good about life lately. And yet I have so much to be thankful for. I don't get it. Am I missing something somewhere?"

"Probably not," Ammon said gently. "It sounds to me like your head's screwed on straight, and your testimony is strong. Just for the record, I agree with you about the money thing. I was certainly not raised with wealth, but we always had sufficient for our needs. We were taught that working hard and paying tithes and offerings, along with the correct attitude, would always make it possible for us to have what was needed, and to even be able to enjoy the good things of the world. I know that to be true."

After a moment of silence, Allison said, "Thank you."

"For what?"

"For listening. And for saying something that makes me feel like I'm not the only one in the world who feels the way I do. I mean . . . I know Sariah feels that way. I should have guessed that her brothers would, too."

"Well, Mosiah doesn't necessarily agree. But I think he'll figure it out eventually. Sally's already teaching him about what's important in life."

Ammon went on to tell her a little about their different personalities and struggles. Mosiah had been a little more headstrong than his brothers, though he was still a good man and had served a mission and married in the temple.

Ammon spoke of his close relationship with his siblings; how they had supported each other through missions and college. He talked of how he enjoyed working with Helaman, and went on to explain that he had worked construction to earn his way through college, majoring in business management. When Ammon got the degree, he realized that he really enjoyed construction and he was good at it. So he applied what he had learned and became a contractor, and Helaman had been a great support in the business.

He emphasized again how his family had always been there for him. He believed that families were made to help each other through their struggles. It was evident that Ammon had a deep love for his family, just as Sariah did. Allison's mind wandered to her own family, and she wondered if her attempts to be independent were a little out of balance.

"What are you thinking?" he asked.

"About home."

"Why *don't* you go home for Christmas?" he asked.

"Well, part of the reason was that I couldn't afford to take the time off work, but . . ."

"But that's irrelevant now."

"Right."

"So, why not?"

Attempting to explain it simply, she said, "I just know I'm supposed to stay here. I don't know why, but I learned a long time ago not to dispute the answers to prayers."

Ammon gave her a warming smile that made her feel a little better. "Then I'm certain there's a reason," he said.

Allison nodded and looked away, wishing she could get rid of this lonely ache. Here she was, having good conversation with someone who was quickly becoming a friend to her, and all she could do was long for home.

"Hey, are you hungry?" he asked.

"Yes, actually. Do we have any more of that canned soup you're so good with?"

"I was thinking more of going out."

"*Out?*"

"No," he chuckled, "I mean . . . I'll go out, and bring something back."

"Okay," she agreed.

"Any preferences?"

"Not really. I'll eat just about anything within normal parameters."

"I'll hurry," he said and left the apartment. Allison noticed as the door came open that it was snowing. She peeked out the window as he drove away and groaned to see how deep the snow was. Well, that was one advantage of not having to work. She decided to enjoy her opportunity to stay in while it lasted.

Allison took more medicine and decided she felt good enough to take a quick shower before Ammon returned. Just being clean helped her feel a little better. She put on a clean sweat suit and snuggled back onto the couch just a few minutes before he came back with taco salads.

While they were eating, Ammon started talking about his feelings on many issues where gospel principles seemed to get tangled into worldly beliefs, and how many good members of the Church seemed to struggle with gray areas. He talked about observing the Sabbath, the effect of the media, and staying morally clean. He strongly expressed his beliefs about morality, admitting that he had group dated for the most part prior to his mission, and he'd always tried hard to keep himself worthy, knowing that it would affect his marriage one day. Allison couldn't deny feeling a little uncomfortable on that one point, recalling the rebellious period she'd gone through before her mission. Although she had seen the repentance process through years ago, and she knew her slate was technically wiped clean, she wondered if her past would ever stop hanging over her. Feeling as comfortable with Ammon as she did, she was tempted to ask his views on such an issue. But the probable embarrassment of admitting to her mistakes overruled her curiosity, and she said nothing.

Ammon went on in the same vein, coming back to the money issue she had started on earlier and sharing his feelings about it from a more personal perspective. He admitted that he had been engaged once to a beautiful blonde named Carolyn. But after the engagement, as they had planned the wedding, this woman became so concerned about appearances and material things that Ammon had ended up calling it off.

He told Allison that he admired her attitude, and he reminded her that money problems were one of the greatest causes of divorce. He finished by saying, "It's important for two people to agree on things that affect their lives so much. And since we are taught very specifically how to use money in the Book of Mormon, it stands to reason that such attitudes are basic to our religion."

They talked long after lunch was finished. When the conversation finally ran down, Allison said, "It's nice of Sariah to share her big brother with me, since I don't have one."

Ammon's expression seemed a little odd, but Allison figured that whether or not he appreciated the concept, she was grateful for his friendship at this time.

Chapter Five

"Maybe I should let you rest," Ammon said. "Is there something I can do for you before I go? Do you need anything at the store, or—"

"I think I've got what I need. Thanks anyway. Let me pay you for my lunch," she added, standing up to go get her wallet.

"Lunch is on me," he insisted.

"Okay. Thank you. But I owe somebody for car repairs. If you'll tell me what it—"

"Helaman did the work, and I'll tell you right now that a hug is the most payment he'll take." He stood and put his hand on the doorknob. "I got the parts cheap. It was no big deal."

"If it's no big deal, then let me pay you for them," she retorted.

"You know," he said with serious eyes but a facetious tone, "there's only one problem I see with people who grow up with too much money."

Allison attempted a protest, certain he was somehow mocking her. But he leaned toward her slightly and spoke before she could. "They tend to be too proud to accept help from others graciously. If we were never in need, we would never give others the opportunity to serve."

Allison opened her mouth to speak, but nothing came out. He was right and she knew it. With all her deeply contemplated views about financial matters, she had never considered such a thing before in her life. She was groping for some response when he touched her chin briefly, adding with a smile, "Remember, Allison, nobody can completely make it on their own. We're here to help each other. And it has very little to do with money."

He was gone before she could get a sound out. But his words lingered with her. Ammon Mitchell was not only adorable, he was wise and spiritual. He had to be too good to be true. It seemed that every time she talked to him, she learned something. In her prayers she thanked her Heavenly Father for leading her to Sariah and her family, and for the opportunity she would have to spend Christmas with them. She asked for help in overcoming her homesickness, knowing it was selfish and pointless.

The following day she felt better, but as Ammon had said in reference to Sariah's illness, she felt as if she'd been hit by a truck. She spent the day studying vigorously for her finals, grateful that she had some connections who were keeping her posted on what she had missed in her classes.

Sariah invited Ammon and Helaman over for dinner that evening. Allison enjoyed their time together, but she thought it strange that she and Sariah had lived in the same apartment for over three months before she'd even met her brothers. Now they were around all the time. She reasoned that they had likely been extremely busy with the construction business until this long spell of bad weather had set in.

After dinner, they played *Pictionary* until they were all laughing and teasing each other. Allison thought very little about home.

On Sunday, Allison went to church while it continued to snow off and on, and she forced herself to not study. She felt anxious about her finals, but she knew that concentrating on her spiritual studies on the Sabbath would serve her better in the long run. She was grateful when finals were over at last, and she felt good enough about them to believe that her adherence to the commandment had helped her through.

Knowing that classes were finished and she didn't have a job, Allison got down on her knees and asked if it would be all right to go home for Christmas. It didn't take much to search her feelings and know that nothing had changed. She needed to stay. If only she knew *why*. It just didn't make any sense to her. She reminded herself that she needed to have faith and trust in the Lord.

"Maybe you would have died in a plane crash on the way home," Sariah suggested when Allison reported the current status of her feelings.

"I don't think I like that thought."

"Well, it was just an idea. You may never really know why. Just take it as it comes. And hey, Christmas at Nana's is great. You'll love it."

Allison smiled and had to admit, "I'm sure I will."

Helaman called a while later to tell Sariah that the back roads in Spanish Fork were packed with snow, and they were going sleigh riding. Sariah's excitement seemed a little out of proportion, but Allison willingly went along. She couldn't remember the last time she'd gone sledding.

They walked into Lupe's house to find the old woman bundling up in a coat, gloves, and a long scarf that went over her head and around her throat. Allison was trying to imagine Lupe sledding as the three of them walked out the back door and trudged through the snow.

"The boys are out in the barn," Lupe announced. "Snow can be a trial, but I don't miss the winters when we've had too little to pull out the old sleigh."

Allison followed Sariah and her grandmother into the barn. She froze momentarily from surprise. Then she couldn't help laughing at herself.

"Is something funny?" Helaman asked.

"It's just that . . . I thought you meant . . ." Allison laughed again.

"You mean one of those." Sariah pointed to the wall, where a couple of little sleds were hanging.

"Yeah!" Allison said, then she turned again to the sleigh, now being harnessed to two horses. It had a front and back seat and long, brightly painted runners. Another uncontrollable laugh erupted from Allison's throat as the bells on the harnesses jingled with the horses' restless movement. Allison watched Sariah's brothers working with the animals and felt a certain envy. She couldn't remember the last time she'd touched a horse.

Allison was still admiring the horses when Ammon nudged her. "Are you coming?"

"Of course," she insisted. Helaman had just helped Sariah and Lupe into the backseat and climbed up beside them, tucking a blanket over their laps. She had no choice but to sit in front with Ammon, who was apparently driving. He helped her up and pointed to the folded blanket on the seat, which she spread over their laps. He made a clicking noise with his tongue, and the horses pulled the sleigh onto the starlit path. Since the clouds had cleared, the temperature had dropped. But oh, what a beautiful night!

"Where are Mosiah and Sally?" Sariah asked.

"Sally wasn't feeling well, bless her heart," Lupe reported. "Perhaps they'll have another chance."

Allison felt as if she were in the center of some Christmas card photograph as they moved noiselessly through quiet back streets, observing the homes illuminated with brightly colored lights, and decorated trees shining in the windows. While she had become accustomed to living in Australia, where Christmas came in the middle of summer, she had to admit that the snow certainly added a magic to the season she'd never bothered to appreciate before.

"Enjoying yourself?" Ammon asked quietly.

"Is it that obvious?" she replied.

He smiled. "Yeah, it's obvious."

Allison became preoccupied with Ammon's hands at the reins. Growing up with horses, she had come to recognize a person's ability to handle them. And Ammon knew what he was doing. She noticed his gloves, made of fine leather, but thin with a couple of small holes. She felt an unexplainable quiver as she noticed the way his hands filled them out so nicely. She concluded that

57

being near horses again made her feel somehow more alive than she had felt in a long while.

A few minutes later, Allison asked, "May I?" She nodded toward the reins.

"Have you ever done this before?"

"Not exactly, but . . . I think I can handle it."

Allison felt a tingle go through her as Ammon carefully guided the reins into her hands. Holding them made her realize that her own gloves weren't so good, either. She drove the team for several minutes before she returned the control to Ammon. The excursion got better when Sariah started singing carols, and the others joined in.

The cold finally forced them to go back. Ammon offered to take care of the horses if Helaman would help Lupe into the house and see that she got warmed up. Sariah went with her grandmother, but Allison felt compelled to linger with the horses. While Ammon was unhooking the harnesses, she nuzzled close to one of the animals and pressed a hand down its muscled neck.

"You like horses," Ammon observed.

Allison laughed, mostly at the image that popped into her head of how her parents might have reacted to such a statement. "I like horses," she said.

"Is it funny?"

"My family's business is horses. It's one of the reasons I miss being at home. For many years, my *life* was horses."

Ammon made a noise to indicate he was impressed. "What exactly does your family do?"

"Breed, train, you name it. We specialize in horses for racing." She gave a sad smile and added, "My dream once was to become a jockey."

"Why didn't you?"

Allison shuffled her boot over the ground. "A back injury; a riding accident, ironically. I was told that I would never be able to withstand riding professionally."

Allison heard an empathetic sigh. "That must have been tough."

"Yeah," she chuckled to lighten the tension. "I must admit it threw my life off a little, but I adjusted . . . eventually."

Little was said as she helped Ammon see that the horses were cared for. Then they walked into the house, where Lupe had hot cocoa waiting. Allison enjoyed the evening thoroughly, but when they went to leave, her car was stuck in the snow. Helaman and Ammon attempted to push the car out, but one wheel had gone into some kind of hole and it wouldn't budge.

"I could pull it out with the truck," Ammon said, "but it would be a lot easier in daylight. Why don't I take you ladies home, and you can get your car tomorrow."

Allison was tired and agreed without argument. With Ammon's offer to help, she didn't feel any anxiety over it. On the way home, she contemplated writing a letter to her mother. She wanted to tell her about the sleigh ride, and how much she was growing to care for Sariah's family. She figured that even if her mother didn't get the letter before Christmas, it would make Allison feel better to write it. Phone calls were nice, but like Emily often said, a letter was something to keep.

Ammon walked with them into the apartment, where the phone was ringing. Sariah grabbed it and handed it to Allison. "It's for you."

Thinking it might be her mother, she said, "Thanks, I'll take it in my room."

When Allison came out a few minutes later, Sariah was looking through a recipe book while Ammon dug into a cupboard, exclaiming, "I don't *see* any chocolate chips!"

"What's wrong?" Sariah asked when she saw Allison. Ammon turned quickly and bumped his head on the cupboard door.

"Are you all right?" Allison asked.

"I'm fine," he insisted, rubbing a spot on his black, curly head. "What's wrong?" he repeated Sariah's question.

"My grandmother died this evening."

"I'm so sorry," Sariah said and stood to hug Allison. "Are you okay?"

"Oh, yeah. It's not really unexpected. The funeral is on the twenty-second."

"Are you going?"

"I think I should." She sighed and added, "Maybe this is why I wasn't supposed to go home for Christmas."

Allison found the phone book and spent the next two hours trying to get a flight to Arizona. Ammon and Sariah had baked cookies, cleaned up the kitchen, and played two rounds of Scrabble before she finally declared, "There is *no* flight available to or from *anywhere* in Arizona before Christmas!" She pressed her head into her hands and sighed. "I guess I'll just have to drive. I really feel like I should go." She looked up at Ammon and asked, "Do you think you can get my car out early so I can get the oil changed and—"

"You can't drive that thing to Arizona right now. Have you heard the weather report?"

"No, why?" Allison asked, wondering what else could go wrong.

"Well, it could get bad." Ammon almost sounded angry. "You can't drive that weightless piece of metal with lousy tires from here to Arizona with winter storm warnings."

"I'll go with her," Sariah insisted.

"What difference is that going to make?"

"She won't be alone!"

"Oh, then you can be *two* stranded or dead women instead of one. And that little heap you drive is worse than hers."

"All right, *big brother*," Sariah said with sarcasm, "just what do you think our options are? If we need to get there, and we pray about it, the Lord will help us."

"Hey," Allison interjected, "this is my problem, you know. You guys don't have to—"

Ammon looked alarmed for some reason. "One day, young lady, you're going to learn you're not required to get through this life single-handedly." He turned to Sariah and added, "And *you* need to realize that there is *always* an option. *I* will drive the two of you to Arizona, because I have absolutely nothing better to do with my life, and I actually own a vehicle that will withstand a lot more weather than either of yours. Praying for the Lord's help still wouldn't hurt."

Allison and Sariah both gaped at Ammon, then at each other, then at Ammon again. Sariah was the first to find her voice. "Are you sure?"

"Sure I'm sure." Ammon pushed his hands into the back pockets of his jeans. "When do we leave?"

Allison sat down, feeling suddenly overwhelmed with emotion. She didn't know if it was her grandmother's death, or the evidence of the Lord looking out for her. Or maybe it was the reality that Sariah and her family were so willing to help the Lord in looking out for her. Or perhaps it was the evidence that Ammon was right—again. She couldn't get through life single-handedly, and for some reason she was having a difficult time getting through her pride enough to see that. Or maybe it was a little bit of everything. She managed to hold the tears back while they discussed when to leave in order to get there in plenty of time for the viewing. She told them she'd cover expenses with the money she would have spent on the flight. Then she thanked them and went to her room to cry.

Chapter Six

Ammon came early to pick up Sariah and Allison for their quick trip to Arizona. While he stood in the back of the truck to adjust the luggage, tying it beneath a tarp to keep it dry, Sariah went back into the apartment to make certain the furnace had been turned down, and to lock the door.

"You're really very sweet to do this, Ammon," Allison said. "In fact, you've been so nice to me, I hardly know what to say. You're kind of like the big brother I never had."

Ammon stopped in the middle of tying a knot, as if he'd been freeze-dried. Allison vaguely recalled the scowl he'd given her the last time she'd mentioned something about him being her brother. She was wondering what sensitive point she had struck unknowingly when he glanced up with eyes that seemed to see right through her.

"Did I say something wrong?" she asked when his expression became too intense to ignore.

Ammon let go of the ropes and leaned both hands on the edge of the truck. His gaze deepened as he said,

"I have no desire to be your brother, Allison."

For a moment, everything seemed to stop. It wasn't so much what Ammon had said, as the look in his eyes when he'd said it, that finally made his implication sink in. Allison felt her face go warm and she turned away, struggling to hide her surprise. Or was it embarrassment? While she was trying to digest the fact that Ammon Mitchell had just admitted he was attracted to her, a quickening of her heart seemed to affirm something she had apparently been oblivious to.

"Oh, help," she murmured under her breath.

"Did you say something?" he asked. She turned to look at him, almost hoping to find some evidence that she had imagined the whole thing. But his dark eyes sparkled with unmasked adoration. Had it been there all along and she'd been too dense to see it? Or had he been guarded until now? She shook her head in an attempt to answer his question. He held her gaze unflinchingly, and something intangible yet undeniably real left her powerless to resist. She was struggling to come up with something to say when Sariah appeared, announcing that she was ready. Ammon finished tying the tarp down and got in the truck. Allison didn't know whether to be thrilled or terrified when Sariah urged her in first. She had no choice but to sit next to Ammon—or look like a fool trying to avoid it.

The long drive commenced in silence. Sariah read. Ammon drove. Allison's mind whirled like a tornado. She contemplated the time she and Ammon had spent together over the past several days. Was she so *dense*?

As the miles flew behind them, Allison felt the silent tension deepen, especially when Sariah put her book aside and fell asleep. She noticed that Ammon was chewing gum, and occasionally she caught a vague scent of wintergreen. Actually, he *always* chewed gum, she realized. Feeling even more tense, she glanced at her wrist, then remembered that she'd lost her watch and hadn't had a chance to replace it.

Ammon showed her his watch. She took note of the time and nodded, embarrassed by the evidence that he was very aware of her actions.

Ammon finally broke the silence. "You seem . . . uptight."

Oh, great, she thought. *Now he's expecting me to talk about this.* She reminded herself to be honest.

"I'm just trying to figure out exactly what you're implying you want to be, if it's not my brother." Ammon showed a brief, crooked smile that eased the tension somewhat. "A friend?" she guessed.

"Yes, but . . ." he drawled.

"But?" she echoed. Her heart nearly pounded out of her chest when he took her hand, threading her fingers between his, and briefly pressed it to his lips.

He glanced at her, then back to the road, saying quietly, "If I'm out of line here, Allison, just say so. I'm not necessarily good at expressing my feelings. Maybe I'm just too cautious. But the truth is, I haven't been able to stop thinking about you since the moment I laid eyes on you."

Allison heard herself take a sharp breath. She tried again in the ensuing silence to recall all the times they'd been together: skating, his grandmother's house, the trip from the airport, the sleigh ride. He'd helped with her car, taken care of her when she was sick. Had she been so blind to the silent messages he'd been sending? Had she missed the intent of his attention? While she was trying to make sense of it, something unexplainably warm slowly filled her, bathing every nerve in serenity. The sensation was so thoroughly consuming that she couldn't hold back the tears that slid down her face, as if this feeling had nowhere else to go. She discreetly wiped at them with the hand that Ammon wasn't holding, but she felt certain he noticed.

Nothing more was said for several miles. While Allison's head swam with a thousand thoughts, Sariah began to snore softly, and Ammon chuckled. "I didn't realize my sister snored," he said.

"Only when she has a cold," Allison said.

The tension seemed to ease a little, and as the miles passed Allison began to feel sleepy herself. She didn't realize how drowsy she was until her head bobbed up. Without saying a word, Ammon shifted his arm around her, urging her head to his shoulder. "Wake me if I snore," she said, relishing the security that suddenly seemed to surround her.

The next thing she knew, Ammon was carefully easing his arm from around her. "Sorry," he said as she sat up straight and tried to orient herself, "I need this hand to shift." She realized they were exiting the freeway. "We need some gas," he said, "and something to eat probably wouldn't hurt."

On the next stretch of the trip, Sariah read a quiz out of a fashion magazine entitled "How compatible are you and your sweetheart at Christmas?" Allison groaned inwardly, wondering if Sariah had any clue about the changes occurring between her and Ammon.

"First question," Sariah said. "'Do you prefer spending Christmas, A: at Disneyland, B: in a secluded mountain cabin, or C: with a big family gathering?'"

"C!" Allison and Ammon both said at the same time. He smiled in her direction, and she attempted to quell a rush of butterflies.

"Next question," Sariah continued. "'You consider the ideal gift from your sweetheart to be, A: something expensive, B: something you need, or C: something homemade.'"

While Allison thought clearly *B*, she held her tongue. Ammon glanced at her as if he was attempting to read her mind, then he said, "B."

Sariah's questions went on, with Allison and Ammon answering nearly everything the same. She wondered if Sariah was as oblivious to the romantic tension as she seemed to be.

"Last question," Sariah announced, and Allison sighed audibly. "'If you were snowed in for the holiday with your sweetheart, what would you consider most important to have with you to make it a good Christmas? A: decorations, lights, Christmas tree, B: Christmas dinner with all the trimmings, C: each other, or D: the gifts?'"

"Most definitely C," Ammon said, winking discreetly at Allison while Sariah continued to read in silence. She then announced the results, declaring that Ammon and Allison were extremely compatible—at least when it came to celebrating Christmas.

"Well, that certainly makes it nice," Ammon said facetiously, "since we're spending Christmas together." He smirked, and Allison resisted the urge to call him a rogue.

Beyond stopping for meals and gas, they drove straight through and got a motel room when they arrived at their destination in the middle of the night. Allison shared a bed with Sariah, and hardly had a minute to think about Ammon in the other bed before she fell asleep from exhaustion. Late the following morning, they finally got moving enough to get something to eat, then they went to David and Louise's home. Ammon remained courteously aloof, but there was an ever-present tension between them that made it impossible for Allison to ignore what was happening.

Allison was pleased with the way Louise drew Ammon and Sariah in, making them feel at home. Christmas preparations were evident in the home, giving it a coziness that hadn't been so evident on Allison's previous visit. There were a few other relatives going in and out, and Allison enjoyed getting to know some cousins she couldn't recall ever meeting. They visited for quite a while, discussing the funeral plans that had been made. Occasionally Louise shed a stray tear, while David mostly read the newspaper or watched sports on television. Allison still found his resemblance to her father a bit unsettling.

When the somber mood of the house began to feel stifling, Allison was relieved to hear her cousin ask if anyone wanted to play some casual basketball in the driveway. They decided to go girls against the boys, even though the boys were outnumbered five to three. Allison enjoyed the exercise almost as much as she appreciated the laughter, and she actually found her cousins to be a lot of fun as they joked and teased throughout the game. She often caught Ammon's eye, unable to deny a sparkle there that made something inside her flutter.

The boys won, twenty-seven to nineteen, then they all went inside where Louise had lemonade, raw vegetables and dip, and sloppy joes waiting. After they ate and helped clean up the kitchen, Allison and her traveling companions returned to their motel room to get cleaned up and dress for the viewing. Allison was the first to shower, then she did her hair and makeup at the mirror across from the beds while Sariah showered.

While she was trying not to feel uncomfortable, well aware that Ammon was watching her, he appeared behind her in the mirror and said, "You really are adorable, you know that?"

Allison attempted to ignore the quiver sparked by his compliment. She smiled at his reflection and said, "I get the feeling you're trying to tell me something."

"You think?" he said facetiously.

She was tempted to tell him to stop beating around the bush and just get to the point, but she was a little afraid of what that point might be.

Through the viewing, Allison mingled and made an effort to get to know the many relatives she'd likely not seen since her own father's funeral, few of whom she remembered. She'd insisted that Sariah and Ammon didn't need to attend the viewing and funeral, but they hovered nearby in silent support, and she couldn't help being grateful.

Allison cried a little when she first saw her grandmother in the casket. Their relationship had been distant and a little bizarre, but Joan was her grandmother nevertheless. The reality of death was itself a little unsettling, and memories of her father's passing crowded into her mind. At one point in the evening, she pretended to be admiring the floral arrangement with a card from her family, while a rush of tears just seemed to come from nowhere. She was startled when Ammon touched her shoulder.

"Are you okay?" he asked gently. His breath smelled of wintergreen.

"Isn't it customary to cry at funerals?"

"Yes, but . . ."

"Oh, I'll be all right," she sniffled and dabbed at her eyes, hoping her mascara wasn't running.

"It's difficult losing someone you love," he stated.

"I cared for my grandmother," she admitted. "But it's hard to say if I really loved her; at least not the way I would have liked to. I'm not certain I ever had the chance—not to mention the fact that she was a difficult woman to love."

"Then why are you crying?"

It was easy for Allison to explain. "I've been thinking about my father. I was nine when he died. I can't help remembering his funeral, and I wonder how it all affected me at the time. I think I struggled with his death for years." She chuckled and sniffled at the same time. "I don't know. Maybe I'm still struggling with it."

"Why is that?" Ammon asked, and Allison looked into his empathetic dark eyes. He really cared.

"I guess it's one of those gray things. He wasn't such a bad guy, but I have very clear memories of hearing him speak to my mother in a way that was degrading and less than kind. I guess I've always felt a little sad for him. I know his upbringing had some difficulties. And I wonder where he stands now."

Ammon was silent for a long moment, and she was surprised to feel his arm come around her shoulders with a quick, reassuring squeeze. She was reminded of their conversation on the way home from the airport, even before he said, "Isn't it wonderful to have the gospel, and to know that our Savior understands those gray things, even if we don't?" Allison met his eyes again, marveling at the way he could express thoughts that she had difficulty defining. He smiled and added, "In a way, isn't that what Christmas is all about?"

Allison nodded and smiled. "Yes, I believe you're right. Thank you. I think I feel better."

As he pulled away, Allison touched his arm to look at his watch. "At least this will be over soon," she said. Ammon smiled and looked into her eyes with silent messages that provoked a secret thrill.

The viewing ended a little after eight, and Louise invited them back to the house for brownies and milk. They went to the motel first to change into comfortable clothes, saving their dress clothes for the funeral. Long after everyone had had their fill of dessert, Allison noticed Sariah visiting intently with one of her cousins, but she couldn't see Ammon. When he didn't show up for a while, she wandered outside to find him shooting baskets in the driveway by a light shining from the back porch. She was tempted to ask him what he was doing out here all alone. Instead, she rushed past him and stole the ball as it bounced off the rim. She dribbled around him while he laughed, then she aimed and missed.

"Care for a little one-on-one, Mitchell?" she asked as she caught the ball and dribbled some more.

"You're on," he said, stealing the ball from her and scoring two points with little trouble. Allison managed to hold her own pretty well. He was taller, but she was

71

quick and agile. Then she wondered if he was just being easy on her. She was preparing for a long shot when his arms came around her from behind, and she dropped the ball.

"Foul!" she laughed, trying to ignore the quickening of her heart. "Don't you know this isn't a contact sport, Mitchell?"

"Basketball or matters of the heart?" he asked in a soft voice just behind her ear. He turned her to face him with his hands at her shoulders. All humor fled behind the intensity in his eyes. "You did say we were playing one-on-one," he observed subtly, the fervor in his eyes deepening.

Allison didn't have time to even squeeze a sound between her lips before he kissed her. Finding no will or reason to protest, she readily admitted that this was likely one of the most impressionable moments of her life. Their eyes met for just a second before he kissed her again—a kiss unlike anything she had ever experienced before. It was as meek as it was profound. Never before had she considered the possibility that a kiss could be spiritual; but this one was.

"Ammon," she whispered as their lips parted. Then she touched his face when she hadn't even contemplated wanting to.

"I love you, Allison," he said, pressing a hand to her cheek. "I can't tell you why or how. I only know that I do."

It took a moment for his words to sink in. Then she stepped back and took in a deep breath of reality.

"Did I say something wrong?" he asked, vulnerability showing in his eyes.

Allison chuckled and looked down. She shook her head, reminding herself to be honest—with herself as well as him.

"You're scaring me, Ammon. You know practically nothing about me. How can you—"

"I know a lot about you, Allison," he said in a tone that indicated her confession had not ruffled him. "I know your beliefs and convictions are real. I know you love life and you care about the things that really matter. I know how I feel about you."

Allison hated to burst the bubble he was creating around them, but she couldn't help contemplating the previous disillusionments in her life. Looking him in the eye, she asked, "Is that enough?"

"Enough for what?" he asked, a trace of mischief in his eyes.

Allison felt a little like she was being put on the spot, but she cleared her throat and reminded herself that he had just admitted he loved her. *Her!* She was not being presumptuous to say, "Enough to base a relationship on."

"Allison," he touched her chin and stepped closer, "I believe that two people who are truly committed to the gospel and live it can be happy together. Although, I'd like to add that being attracted to each other doesn't hurt any. *I* certainly don't have a problem with either one."

Allison absorbed the implication and replied, "Neither do I, for that matter." It came out in a breathy, almost dreamy whisper, and he smiled. She took a deep breath and asked, "Are you trying to propose to me, Ammon Mitchell?"

He chuckled and glanced down briefly. When he looked back up, the intensity in his eyes had deepened further. "Yes, actually, I believe I am."

The reality sent Allison's heart racing. She heard a little gasping sound come out of her mouth and turned her back to him, as if looking elsewhere would help her see things more clearly. While she was fumbling to tell him that she needed time to think about this, he spoke gently behind her ear. "Of course, there's no hurry. You can let that idea settle. If it's something you might consider, just let me know. In the meantime . . ." He kissed the side of her face and eased his arms around her.

"In the meantime?" she echoed when he didn't finish. He kissed her cheek again, and she briefly became lost in the sensation.

"I'll just keep spending every minute with you that I can respectably spend. You're simply too irresistible."

Allison turned again to look at him, admitting, "I was just thinking the same about you."

She didn't hesitate to press her arms around his shoulders when he kissed her again. Somewhere in the midst of it, Sariah's voice could be heard saying, "What is this? My brother making moves on my best friend?"

Allison turned in embarrassment to see Sariah standing on the porch, her arms folded. It was difficult to tell if she was amused or disgusted. Ammon was apparently unconcerned as he laughed and hugged Allison tightly. "You'd better believe it," he said.

Allison could hardly sleep that night as a thousand thoughts tumbled through her head. While Sariah snored softly through her stuffy nose, Allison's mind jumped from death and funerals, to the feeling that something had been left undone with her grandmother, to the reality that Ammon Mitchell was sleeping in the same room. His confessions of love rang through her head, sending fresh tingles of excitement to her every nerve. Contemplating her disappointments in the past, she wondered if she was being too hasty. But it didn't take long to recount their conversations and the evidence she had of his values and beliefs. And, all things considered, she had never felt *anything* to compare to the way Ammon made her feel. How could it not be right?

With her thoughts swirling endlessly, Allison nearly resigned herself to just staying awake the remainder of the night. Then she heard Ammon whisper through the darkness, "Allison, are you awake?"

"Like a night owl," she replied.

"There's something I need to say," he went on, "and since my sister is snoring, I assume this is as good as private."

"I'm listening," she said, keeping an ear tuned to the indication that Sariah was still sleeping.

"Well . . . I've been thinking a lot about . . . well, when things didn't work out with Carolyn, I just kind of stopped dating altogether. I basically told the Lord that I wasn't sure I had what it took to find the right woman, and I was putting it in his hands. Of course, I know that he expects us to make an effort, and maybe deep inside I held myself back because I was scared. I guess what I'm trying to say is . . . I wasn't expecting this to happen. And even more so, I'm amazed, and . . . may I say, humbled . . . by the way I feel . . ."

The crack in his voice spurred an unexpected rush of emotion in Allison. She was warmed and surprised by

75

the tears that leaked out of the corners of her eyes, running into her hair.

"I think," he went on, his voice more steady now, "that your coming into my life has taught me something about faith. I realize now that in spite of my weaknesses, in my heart a part of me truly believed the Lord would find the woman I was meant to spend eternity with, and he did. The moment I saw you, I could almost hear him saying, 'Now it's up to you, kid. The ball's in your hands.' Am I making any sense?"

"Oh, yes," Allison said with conviction, "you're making a great deal of sense; so much sense that I'm . . . *humbled*, myself."

"So, do you think this is real, Allison? I'm not dreaming?"

"If you're dreaming, Ammon, we're both having the same dream."

Allison could barely make out his shadow as he leaned up on one elbow and looked toward her through the darkness. "What are you saying, Allison?" he asked, and she was touched by the hint of vulnerability coming through in his voice.

Allison took a deep breath, knowing there was no use denying it. "I love you, too, Ammon. What I feel with you makes everything I've experienced before in my relationships seem somehow . . . trite." She paused and asked, "Does that make any sense?"

She could almost hear him smile through the darkness. "Oh, it makes perfect sense. When I asked Carolyn to marry me, I believed that what I felt for her was incomparable. I realize now that it was just so . . . I can't explain it."

76

"I think I know what you mean," Allison said. They talked for nearly an hour, then Allison drifted into a contented sleep. She awakened, vaguely aware of the shower running. She felt a kiss on her brow and opened her eyes to see Ammon's smiling face hovering above hers.

"Good morning," he said.

Allison pulled the covers over her head and muttered, "Well, I certainly don't have to fear having you see the real me."

He chuckled, and she stayed under the covers until she knew that Sariah had come out of the bathroom and Ammon was in the shower.

"So, what's up with you and Ammon?" Sariah asked while Allison was gathering her clothes.

Allison wondered where to begin, and came up with an obvious point: at the beginning. "He told me when we were loading up the truck to leave that he had no desire to be my brother. Since then, it's become evident that . . ."

"He's madly in love with you," she provided.

Allison felt warmed just to hear it. "It would seem that way."

"And how do you feel?" Sariah asked.

"I'm afraid I'm sunk. My heart's involved, whether I want it to be or not. I've never felt this way before in my life. It's like . . . as soon as I really stopped to look at it, this big bright light came on inside of me."

"Wow," Sariah said through a lengthy sigh.

Allison felt a little unnerved when Sariah sat weakly on the edge of the bed, staring into space. She wondered if her best friend would somehow disapprove of this relationship. Finally a little laugh erupted from Sariah's mouth, then she looked at Allison, saying, "I can't believe it." Before Allison could question Sariah's feelings, she stood from the bed and put her arms around Allison, hugging her tightly. "There is no one I would rather have as my sister-in-law."

Allison laughed softly, then replied, "Well, we're not married yet. We hardly know each other, when it comes right down to it. I think we need to give it some time."

"Well, if both of you feel as strongly as you say, time probably isn't going to make much difference. If it's right, it's right."

Allison pondered that thought through the funeral, and afterward as they went to the cemetery for the dedication of the grave. An unexpected rush of tears caught Allison as the family began to disperse. She had barely located a tissue in her purse when Ammon's arm came around her, and she found his shoulder conveniently there to absorb her emotion. She cried for only a minute or two, but felt hesitant to move from the comfort of his embrace. She heard Sariah tell her brother she was riding back to the church with some of Allison's cousins. Ammon nodded and tightened his arms around Allison.

"Are you going to be all right?" he asked a minute later.

"Oh, yes," she insisted, wiping at her face.

"Are you thinking about your father, or—"

"That's most of it, I think. Sometimes I wonder if I ever really mourned his death the way I should have. More than anything, I think the whole thing just left me confused."

"Do you want to talk about it?" he asked, walking back toward the truck with his arm around her.

"I'm not sure what to say." She smiled up at him. "Maybe later."

While they were driving back to the church for a luncheon, Allison dug out her wallet to look at a couple of pictures she had tucked behind some other things. When Ammon turned off the truck in the church parking lot, he asked, "What have you got there?"

Allison handed him the first picture. "That's me the Christmas that I was nine. I'm sitting on my father's lap."

"Wow," he said.

"What?"

"You were adorable then, too." Allison laughed softly and he added, "Your father sure looks like his brother."

"Yes, he does. Maybe that's one reason I can't stop thinking about him." Allison impulsively added, "He acted like him, too."

Ammon said nothing, but the sidelong glance he gave her left no doubt that he had noticed David's anti-social behavior and his abrupt, critical manner.

Allison handed him the other picture. "This is from my parents' wedding."

Ammon chuckled. "I could almost believe this is you. You look very much like your mother." He turned to her and smiled. "You're both very beautiful."

"That's what my father says."

"Your father?"

"Michael; my mother's husband."

Ammon nodded. He looked at the pictures again and handed them back. "I'll look forward to meeting them," he said as he opened the door and stepped out. The thought resulted in an unexpected quiver in

Allison's stomach. Maybe not going home for Christmas wouldn't be so bad after all.

When the luncheon was over, relatives hovered at the church building, visiting and reminiscing. Ammon and Sariah were both chatting with Allison's cousins, apparently enjoying themselves. She was feeling a little lost when Louise approached, handing her a pink envelope.

"What is this?" Allison questioned.

Tears brimmed in Louise's eyes as she said, "Your grandmother dictated this to me the morning before she died."

Allison felt suddenly hesitant as she took the envelope, staring at it as if she could read it by osmosis. Before she had a chance to open it, Louise embraced her, saying warmly, "I'm so grateful you came, Allison. You will never know the difference you made . . . for her . . . and for me." She touched Allison's face briefly and slipped away.

Allison stood alone, staring at the envelope for a full minute before she found the courage to slip out and find an empty classroom where she wouldn't be disturbed. With trembling fingers, she opened the letter and began to read.

My dearest Allison,

As my time on this earth is coming to an end, I feel it's important to let you know what is in my heart. Since the time I learned that I would not live much longer, I've been preoccupied with a great deal of fear and confusion. It's difficult to explain, but I want you to know that you were the answer to many prayers. I wanted so badly to understand why so much of my life had been filled with difficulty and unhappiness. And it was your simple words to me that helped some things to finally make sense.

I can't help wishing that I could go back and raise my children again, knowing what I know now. In spite of growing up a member of the Church, and always trying to do the right thing, I can see that in some ways I let my fears rule my beliefs. What I'm trying to say, Allison, is that I have many regrets, but I know now that my Savior atoned for my mistakes, and once I get to the other side, I will be able to make it right. I realize that there are many difficulties and struggles among my posterity, and I wonder how much of it is because of me. I know there's nothing I can do about it after all this time, but I pray that they will be led to the knowledge I have now; that they will be able to make their lives better through living the gospel as it was meant to be lived.

Thank you again for taking the time to come all this way to see me again. You are—and always have been— a very big bright spot in my life. Seeing you, I know that something good has come from me, even if I can't take any credit for the way you've turned out. One day we will be together again.

> *All my love,*
> *Your grandmother, Joan Hall*

Silent tears had streamed down Allison's face as she'd read the letter, and now they suddenly flooded out. She cried without restraint, grateful to be alone. There was no describing the peace she found in her grandmother's words, or the ache she felt in wanting to just hold her one more time and tell her she loved her.

"Are you okay?" Ammon asked, startling her.

Allison turned away, frantically wiping at her tears. "I thought I was alone. How did you find me?"

"Do you want me to leave you alone?" he asked gently.

With a fresh rush of emotion, she admitted, "No."

"I guess that explains how I found you," he said, urging her into his arms. Allison clung to him and cried, feeling as if she'd come home.

Chapter Seven

Once Allison's emotions had settled, she shared the letter with Ammon and expressed her feelings, though it was difficult to describe the depth of peace she felt regarding her grandmother. As Ammon listened and held her hand, she wondered how she had ever managed without him. How quickly life could change!

The drive home to Utah was relatively pleasant, with much less tension than Allison had found on the previous journey. Sariah hardly seemed to notice the way Ammon held Allison's hand, or put his arm around her as she dozed occasionally. He even asked Allison if she would mind driving for a stretch, since he was feeling sleepy.

"How would she dare?" Sariah interjected. "I know this truck cost you a fortune—not to mention that it's a *stick shift*," she finished, as if it were contaminated or something.

Allison chuckled and told Ammon, "I'd be happy to drive if you want me to. I can assure you I've had a good deal of experience with vehicles more ominous than this."

"Really?" Ammon said as he slowed down and pulled off to the side of the highway.

"I did my fair share of work on the ranch in Australia," she said. "Although, over there, we call it a station." They got out and traded places, then she added, putting the truck into gear, "However, the steering wheel was usually on the other side."

While Allison drove, Sariah read and Ammon dozed on her shoulder. He didn't even snore.

They considered driving straight through, but ended up getting a room in St. George, fearing they'd have trouble staying awake otherwise. Ammon offered to take them out for a nice dinner, but Sariah insisted she was exhausted and voted to order a pizza. Ammon declared he would take Allison out and bring back something for Sariah.

Allison enjoyed the evening, especially the way Ammon possessively held her hand, and the mild sparkle she caught in his eyes when he would look at her. While it felt like a first date—and in actuality it was—she found it difficult to comprehend that he had practically proposed to her. A logical part of her attempted to reason that it was all moving too fast, but something deeper and more powerful told her it was right, and no amount of time passing would prove it otherwise. Still, she felt certain that giving these feelings some time, if only to get to know each other better, would be wise.

After they took dinner back to the room for Sariah, Ammon and Allison took a long walk. The warm St. George climate, combined with the Christmas decor scattered about town, pleasantly reminded Allison of home. But instead of homesickness, she felt only peace.

Ammon and Allison talked a great deal about their families and their interests, and she felt increasingly awed by the reality that this man could very well be the center of her future. He kissed her before they went into the motel room, where Sariah was sleeping soundly.

Somewhere in the middle of the night, as Allison contemplated the turn her life was taking, a thought took hold that made her sit bolt upright in bed. Her chest tightened and she pressed her hands there, suddenly finding it difficult to breathe. Like a splash of cold water, the memories of her teenage rebellion came flooding back. The repentance process had been difficult, but complete. She had since gone to the temple and served a worthy mission. But the fact was, she had made some extremely bad choices that had affected her life. And she had fallen in love with a man who had once told her of his personal convictions to remain morally clean. He had saved himself for marriage. Would he possibly want—or deserve—a woman with such an off-color past?

As the memories began to eat away at Allison's conscience, she wished she could have foreseen this moment prior to taking that first sinful step. She likely could have never gone through with it. Why, of all the struggles she might come up against in pursuing a relationship, did this have to come back and haunt her?

As the night wore on, Allison turned her mind to prayer. She contemplated the reality that she was in no way obligated to tell her future spouse about the sins she'd committed during a difficult time in her life. But she wondered if she could live with keeping it to herself. This man had the potential to become her best friend, as well as her husband. How could she not share with him such a significant part of her life? It had affected who and what she had become. The experience had, in the long run, strengthened her testimony and her love for the gospel. But could she live with such a secret, fearing it might somehow slip out? Sariah knew the truth about her past; could Allison ask her to never share it with her brother, to always be on guard against some hint of it coming to the surface? Thoughts assaulted her of Ammon's possible anger and resentment in discovering he'd married a woman with a less than noble past.

By dawn, Allison came to the conclusion that she had to tell him. She contemplated waiting until they were more comfortable with each other, but as she thought it through and prayed about it, she knew it wouldn't be fair—to either of them—to pretend that everything was all right when it wasn't. If Ammon Mitchell couldn't accept her, along with her past, it would be better to find out now; then they could both move on.

She had almost drifted off to sleep when she heard Ammon going in to take a shower. Sariah moaned herself awake and began gathering her things, while Allison pretended to be asleep.

When Sariah got into the shower and Ammon was combing back his wet hair, Allison sat up in the bed and pulled the covers up to her chin. *Tell him now*, she thought. But Sariah would only be out of the room for a matter of minutes, and the three of them had a long drive ahead of them. No, she needed more time and more privacy.

Something ironically painful tugged at her heart when Ammon turned and grinned at her. "Good morning, gorgeous," he said. She only scowled at him and he added, "What's the matter? Have a bad night?"

"I didn't sleep much, actually," she said.

"Is something wrong?" he asked, perception seeping into his dark eyes.

Allison took a deep breath. "Just a lot on my mind," she insisted with a smile. She was relieved when Sariah came out of the bathroom and she could escape into the shower. After a quick breakfast, they were on their way.

During the drive, Sariah began talking with her brother about the Christmas celebrations waiting for them at home. Allison was surprised to realize that today was actually December twenty-third. She'd been so consumed with the funeral and the travel that time had slipped past her. They talked about the way they traditionally spent the night of Christmas Eve at their grandmother's home, and Sariah insisted that Allison join them. "You never know how early the fun's going to start," she said with a little laugh. "If you don't spend the night there, you'll miss out."

Ammon smiled warmly at Allison, which provoked a quiver of excitement, dampened only slightly by the reality of what she needed to talk to him about.

It occurred to Allison that since she was spending the entire holiday with Sariah's family, she should get some gifts for them. She concluded that a shopping trip would be in order once she got home.

The climate changed drastically between St. George and Cedar City, where the snow began to fall. Going over the Beaver mountain pass, it became so bad that Allison got downright scared.

"Nervous?" Ammon said coolly, his eyes tuned keenly to the road, both hands firmly gripping the wheel.

"Whatever gave you that idea?" she retorted.

He glanced quickly down to his leg, then to her face. He smirked, then turned back to the road. Only then did Allison realize she'd been squeezing his thigh so tightly she'd probably left fingerprints.

"Sorry," she muttered and folded her arms abruptly.

Ammon chuckled. "We're going to be fine."

"Well, I'm glad you think so." Sariah, too, was obviously tense. "I've never seen snow like this in my life."

"I'm just grateful we're not driving one of our stupid little cars," Allison said.

"Amen," Ammon murmured.

They drove mostly in silence while Allison prayed in her mind. She began to relax as she observed Ammon's confidence. He was obviously a skilled driver, and his vehicle handled the snow well. She sighed audibly as the unending white shroud surrounding them began to dissipate. Gradually it merged into a sleety rain, and the visibility increased.

"I'm sure glad you and your truck came along," Allison admitted when the worst was behind them.

"So am I," he said with warmth.

As Utah Valley came closer, Sariah asked Allison what her plans were for the rest of the day.

"I need to do some shopping. Do you want to come along?"

"I'd love to, but I've got to put some hours in at work so I can get off early tomorrow." She glanced toward Ammon and added, "But I'd bet ten dollars that my brother would like to go."

Allison felt a mixture of emotions from his smile. "Only if you want me to, of course," he said.

"Oh, that would be fine," she replied. "I could probably use your opinion."

Ammon dropped the girls off at their apartment and unloaded their luggage, saying he'd be back in a couple of hours to get Allison and take her to the mall. He kissed her quickly while Sariah was in the other room.

"Thank you again," Allison said quietly.

"It was my pleasure." He grinned and squeezed her hand. "I don't think any excursion has ever been so rewarding."

Allison managed a smile, hoping he would still feel the same way after they had a chance to talk.

Allison put off unpacking, since she wanted to get a gift for Ammon, and he would be with her later. She asked Sariah for a few suggestions then hurried out, needing to be back before he returned. Pushing her way through the crowded mall corridor, she prayed silently for some guidance, wanting to get him something appropriate for their newfound relationship; something that would let him know she cared without being too presumptuous. Recalling the thin, well-worn gloves she'd seen him wear when they'd gone sleigh riding, she found a similar pair. Pulling them onto her hands, she smiled at how huge they looked on her. A warm tingle encompassed her to imagine his hands giving them life. The tingle increased as she recalled the tender way he often held her hand. She marveled at how familiar it had become to her in so short a time.

Allison then picked out a tie, covered with colorful hammers and nails—perfect for a contractor, she thought. At a candy store, she bought several packages of the type of gum he chewed, and had them wrapped in fine gold foil with a deep green bow.

Allison was only home long enough to freshen up a little before Ammon came to pick her up. She endured the rush of butterflies triggered by just seeing him, and gladly took his hand as they walked out to the truck. It began to snow again as he drove toward the mall and talked about his parents' arrival from Oregon earlier that day.

"It must have been great to see them," she said, briefly longing for home.

"Yeah," he admitted. "It's been a while." He smiled and added, "They're looking forward to meeting *you*."

"What did you tell them?" She couldn't help feeling a little alarmed.

Ammon chuckled. "I told them I was madly in love with a woman I had every hope of marrying. Or did you want me to lie?"

"No, of course not. But . . . perhaps you could have broken it more . . . delicately."

"I'm just trying to keep up with my feelings," he said in a voice that warmed Allison.

"I'm not sure that's possible," she replied, and he smiled again.

"Where to first?" he asked, turning into the mall parking lot.

"Park close to something to eat," she said. "I'm starving."

"Good plan," he said.

They shared a Chinese combination dinner, and laughed over the absurd fortunes in their cookies. Ammon kept his arm around her as they perused the mall along with what seemed like ten million other last-minute shoppers.

Allison appreciated Ammon's taste when he helped her pick out simple, appropriate gifts for his family. He tried to help pay for them, but she was insistent, and he was gracious. Christmas music was floating in the air, and the magic of the Christmas spirit began to surround them as they sat for a while on a bench. She felt much the same way she had during their sleigh ride. The bustle of shoppers and elaborate decor seemed like some kind of three-dimensional Christmas card, with her and Ammon at the center, holding hands and sharing the newness of these feelings, which were unlike anything she had ever known.

On the way home, Allison rested her head on his shoulder. The snow was falling in large, artful flakes, and Christmas music played on the stereo.

"This has got to be the best Christmas of my life," Ammon said, pressing a brief kiss into her hair.

Allison chuckled warmly. "Yes, I believe you're right—even if I couldn't go home."

Ammon tightened his arm around her. "I'm glad you didn't."

She enjoyed the serenity surrounding her—until she remembered there was something she needed to tell him. She sat up straight so quickly that it startled him.

"Are you all right?" he asked.

"Yes, I just . . ." She couldn't finish. She briefly wondered if she was on the wrong track. Should she even tell him? Or would it jeopardize what they were just discovering between them? It only took a second to know that she *had* to tell him. She'd thought all of this through last night, and she had prayed about it. Perhaps for some people, telling a prospective spouse of such things wouldn't be so relevant. But for her, she knew it was right, and it simply had to be done.

"You just what?" he asked, startling her.

Allison turned toward him, noting the concern that creased his brow. She wondered if she should wait until after Christmas, but something inside told her it just needed to be done. Once she had it over with, she could stop dreading it.

"I . . . uh . . ." Silently, Allison prayed for help. "I . . . need to tell you something."

She sensed his concern increasing. "Okay," he drawled. When she said nothing more, he added, "Now . . . or next year?"

"Perhaps it should wait until next year," she said, attempting to lighten the mood. But he didn't even crack a smile.

"But I'm assuming from the way you're torturing your purse that it won't wait that long."

Allison noted the strap wrung tightly around her hands. She unwound it and set it aside vehemently. "No, I don't think it should wait."

Ammon had pulled the truck up in front of the apartment building before Allison said anything more. He shifted into neutral and turned the stereo down, making it clear that he was listening.

Allison cleared her throat self-consciously. "First of all," she began, feeling almost shaky, "let me say that I wouldn't be telling you this if it weren't for the way I feel about you. I'm amazed at how right we seem for each other, and how good it feels to be with you. And it might sound funny, but for me, it means more knowing you were a friend to me first. I would hope we can always be friends—no matter what happens."

Allison avoided looking at him, but she was keenly aware of his growing attentiveness, as if he was beginning to sense the seriousness of what she had to say. He confirmed it when he said, "You're making me nervous, Allison."

"That makes two of us," she said with a tense chuckle. She took a deep breath and continued. "Technically, there is no reason why I should have to tell you this. I simply feel that for me, it has to be done. I can't spend the rest of my life with a skeleton in my closet, fearing you'll discover it. My past is a part of me; it has made me who I am today. It's important that you know why I am the way I am."

Ammon unfastened his seat belt and turned toward her. "Does this have something to do with your father?" he asked gently.

"Indirectly," she said. "As I've gradually come to terms with the mistakes I've made, I believe more and more that my father's death—and the attitudes he had when he was alive—left me with a lot of confusion and hurt that I had trouble facing up to. And maybe even some guilt. I know that sounds funny, for me to feel guilty for things between my parents that had nothing to do with me. But I did. Maybe that's why the things my grandmother said meant so much to me."

"I think I understand," he said. She only hoped he would continue to understand.

"And then . . . I had that riding accident. It just kind of . . . threw me off. My plans for the future were changed. I felt . . . cheated somehow."

Ammon made a noise to indicate he was listening.

"Anyway," she said, then suddenly felt frozen. She

chuckled uncomfortably and emotion caught her voice. "This is really hard for me."

Ammon took her hand. "I'm listening, Allison."

She nodded and attempted to gather her courage. "Ammon," she turned to look at him, lifting her chin with determination, "I need to tell you that there was a time in my life when I was much less than an exemplary Mormon girl. I've talked to Sariah about it." Through a moment of silence Ammon said nothing, so she forced herself to go on. "I got caught up with a shady crowd, and . . . well, I was . . . rebellious. I rebelled against my family . . . my values . . . everything I'd been taught." Still he said nothing, but she could feel the tension deepening. She'd come too far to back off now; she just had to get it over with. She cleared her throat ridiculously loud and turned to look out the window— anywhere but at him.

While she was attempting to gather her words, he said, "How rebellious?"

Allison squeezed her eyes shut and sighed. "I . . . uh . . . I drank some; smoked a little—although I never found much appeal in either one, and my interest faded fast. And . . ." She just couldn't get the words to come together.

"And?" he said when the silence grew miserable.

She uttered a silent prayer and finally just blurted it out. "I had a relationship, Ammon."

Following a full minute of silence, Ammon turned in his seat and abruptly leaned his arms on the steering wheel. Allison's heart pounded so hard she feared he could hear it above the low hum of the truck engine and the soft music playing.

He finally said, "Are you trying to tell me that you were intimate with a man?"

Allison swallowed hard. "That's what I'm trying to tell you."

She heard him let out a long, slow breath, and wished she could see more than the shadow of his expression in the darkness. He chuckled with no trace of humor. It was more a sound of absolute shock. When the silence lengthened, Allison began to ramble. "It was a long time ago, Ammon; before my mission. I've worked it all through. It's in the past. But like I said, it's affected who and what I am. The experience eventually strengthened my testimony and my love for the gospel. I've often wondered if it was just something that needed to happen. Maybe someone stronger than me could have come to terms with my struggles and frustrations without going so low. But I guess I had to figure things out the hard way."

Still he said nothing. When she couldn't bear it any longer, she came right out and asked, "Don't you have anything to say?"

Another of those shocked noises erupted from his lips. He shook his head and looked down. "I . . . don't know what to say. I'm . . . surprised."

Allison reminded herself of her motives as she attempted to digest his reaction. Needing clarification, she stated, "It bothers you."

"Yeah," he said a little too readily, "it bothers me."

She turned away and attempted to keep the tears silent. "Maybe I shouldn't have told you," she said.

"Did you think it would never come up—that I wouldn't notice? Did you think it would never affect *me*?"

"No, Ammon," she snapped, surprised at her own anger. "That's exactly why I felt I *had* to tell you. But I was told by my bishop years ago that my repentance wiped it clean; it's as if it never happened."

"But it *did* happen," he said. "And it *does* matter. You just told me it has affected your life, and it could affect mine. What are you trying to tell me, Allison? If I marry you, is there a chance I could end up getting AIDS or something? Is that what you're trying to say?"

While Allison was appalled at the suggestion, she had to admit he had a right to ask the question. "No, that's not what I'm saying. I had *one* relationship. I was extremely careful. I took every possible precaution. I never did drugs. I was stupid, but I wasn't a total idiot."

Ammon only shook his head and looked away. The ensuing silence clearly indicated a lack of acceptance and approval. She hated the image that appeared in her mind of the countless times in her childhood that she had observed her father subtly degrade her mother with insinuations and implications that were often too gray to define. Ammon in no way reminded her of her father, but the thought spurred Allison's determination to clear the air and know exactly where she stood.

Chapter Eight

Allison took a deep breath and resigned herself to see the conversation through. "If this is something you can't live with, Ammon, then tell me now and get it over with. I brought it up now because I figured if it was going to come between us, I'd rather know before our relationship goes any further."

An unbearable pounding began to gather behind Allison's eyes as the silence persisted. While she ached to have him assure her that he could live with it, that he wouldn't let it come between them, he said nothing. Trying to be appropriately assertive, Allison finally said, "I'm getting the impression that this is *not* something you can live with."

"I didn't say that!"

"You didn't say anything! If I'm assuming wrong, feel free to straighten me out."

Silence.

"Ammon, talk to me."

"I . . . don't know what to say. I'm just . . . really . . ."

"What?" she questioned when he didn't finish.

"I don't know." He shook his head.

Allison took a deep breath in an attempt to turn her anger to compassion. She tried to imagine how he must be feeling, and felt compelled to remind him, "God forgave me for those sins a long time ago, Ammon."

"Yes, well, you just told me it's a part of your life, and if I make you a part of *my* life, then . . ."

Allison's fears turned to anger, rushing in without control. Taking no thought of the results, she blurted out, "What is it, Ammon? Is it too much to take, to contemplate spending the rest of your life with a tainted woman?"

"I did not say that!" he insisted.

"You didn't say otherwise," she snarled. She might have sensed his desire to explain himself if she hadn't been so consumed with her own emotions. "Well, if that's the way it is, then fine." She gathered her packages and moved toward the passenger door. "I was under the impression that you loved me. I was under the impression you were a Christian. Well, when I marry—*if* I marry—it will be to someone who can accept me unconditionally. And if I told him that I had shot drugs with dirty needles, he would still respect me and love me and risk anything to be a part of my life. That's the kind of love I'm holding out for, Mitchell, because that's the kind of love I'm willing to give. I admire and respect your moral convictions, Ammon, I really do. But not any more than I admire what it took for me to pull myself up out of the gutter and find my way back. We've had different lives, different struggles. And you have no right to judge mine. I will not spend the rest of my life feeling like my husband is somehow superior to me because he didn't make the same mistakes. I refuse to apologize for what is long in the past."

She opened the door and got out, struggling to be certain she had everything while she could almost feel steam coming out of her ears. She paused long enough to see Ammon staring straight ahead, his attitude seemingly cold and distant.

"It's been a pleasure, Mr. Mitchell," she finished with sarcasm and slammed the truck door. All the way to the door of her apartment, she kept hoping he would come after her. She imagined him taking hold of her, telling her he loved her, that she'd misunderstood, that he could live with it. But she went into the empty apartment and leaned against the closed door for several minutes before she heard him drive away. When the sound of his truck's diesel engine could no longer be heard, she slumped to the floor and cried. Why hadn't she just gone home for Christmas? Why had she come to Utah in the first place? Why did she ever have to meet Sariah's brothers? And worst of all, why did she have to fall in love with one of them? When the tears finally ran out, she sat alone in the darkness, wondering why she'd been such a fool to make so many rotten choices in her youth. She wished she could go out into the world and personally shake some sense into every smart-mouthed teenager who believed that messing with commandments would never affect their lives. If she had kept herself as chaste as Ammon Mitchell, they could have been happy together.

Allison tried to tell herself that if he was going to have an attitude like that, she didn't *want* a relationship with him. But the harsh truth couldn't be ignored. She was hopelessly in love with him. He had changed her life so quickly, so completely. She wondered if she would ever get over it. She even considered moving back to Australia right after Christmas, if only to avoid ever having to see him again.

She groaned and threw her purse across the room when she remembered that she was supposed to spend Christmas with Ammon's family. The thought made her almost physically sick. She just wouldn't go. It was as simple as that. She would stay right here and pretend that it was just a day like any other day. And as soon as possible, she would get on a plane and go home. She contemplated the prayerful decision she'd made to stay here for Christmas, and began to question her ability to feel the answer to a prayer at all. Of course, it had been good for her to go to her grandmother's funeral, and to see Joan before her death. But that was done, and she could have been on a plane by now.

Realizing that Sariah could come home soon, Allison gathered up her things and took them to her room. She groaned again to look at the gifts she'd bought for the Mitchell family. It was all so stupid that she wanted to scream. She looked at the package her family had sent for Christmas and was tempted to open it now, but she didn't even want to acknowledge that tomorrow was Christmas Eve. Earlier today, she had believed it would be the best Christmas of her life. Now it was the worst. Was that because she'd made mistakes in her youth? Or because Ammon Mitchell was an arrogant, pigheaded . . . She stifled the thought and groaned aloud. He was a good man, and she knew it. Perhaps he had a right to feel the way he did. When she got past all the anger, it just plain hurt to think of having a future without him.

Allison put on her pajamas and lay in the dark long after she heard Sariah come in and go to bed across the hall. She kept hoping the phone would ring. She ached to just talk to him, to have him tell her they could work it out. She could understand that it might take time for him to come to terms with it. But somehow she knew that time wouldn't make a difference. And judging *him* for *his* weaknesses would not do anybody any good.

It took hours for Allison to fall asleep. She woke up late morning with the sun shining brightly through the slats of the window blinds. She could tell without even looking outside that the snow had stopped and the sky was a brilliant blue. But she didn't care. Her grumbling stomach finally urged her to the kitchen, where she found a note from Sariah saying that she was going shopping with her parents and brothers, and she would be back at four to get Allison before going to Lupe's house.

While Allison fixed some toast and orange juice, she rehearsed possible excuses to give Sariah for not attending the Christmas celebration. If Sariah was now with Ammon, maybe she would already know something had happened. Honesty was obviously the best option. The last thing she wanted was to have Sariah get caught in the middle of something so pathetic. She wondered what to do with the gifts she'd purchased for Sariah's family, and decided to wrap them up and send them anyway. She could have her tell them she was sick or something.

Feeling depression sink in, Allison forced herself to some action. She took a long, hot shower, then turned on some loud music to muffle her emotions while she cleaned up her room and washed the dishes.

A pounding at the door sounded faintly through the music, and she hurried to turn the stereo down before she answered it. Her heart quickened at the thought that it could be Ammon, but she was not disappointed to see Sean O'Hara.

"What are you doing here?" she demanded as he stepped in without waiting for an invitation.

"I was getting worried about you," he said as she closed the door behind her. "Your parents called me yesterday when they couldn't get hold of you. They were wondering if you'd returned from the funeral safely. I've tried to call this morning, but—"

"You did?" Then she sighed sheepishly. "Well, I did have the music up a little loud."

Sean smiled, and she had to admit she was glad to see him. He'd been a friend of the family for many years, since her parents had taken him in. His Catholic family had disowned him when he'd joined the Church. Allison knew there had been a time when her parents had hoped that she and Sean would get together, but the feelings just hadn't been there. Sean was now happily married, and much like a brother to her. He kept close touch with her family, and it wasn't the first time they'd sent him to check up on her when they were concerned. She thought of the way Ammon had also been a brother to her and felt a little queasy.

"So, you're alive," he said. "Is everything okay?"

Allison managed a smile. "Yeah, I'm fine."

Sean scowled. "You're lying."

Just her luck, he had to be a psychologist. She swore he could practically read minds.

"Okay, so I'm not fine." It took little prodding for Allison to spill the whole story in a flood of tears as they sat together on the couch. She blessed Sean's insight as he reminded her that what had happened in the past was between her and the Lord. She wondered all over again if it had been right to tell Ammon, or if she should have kept it to herself.

"Well, I think such decisions are personal, Allie," he said. "But for me, I wanted Tara to know." He went on to explain his feelings about it as if they were her own.

Allison felt a little better to recall that Sean had had his own difficult past before he'd joined the Church. But she had to ask, "And what if Tara had rejected you because of it?"

"That's a tough one, Allie. But I think you're right when you say that if he can't accept you as you are, he may not be worth sharing eternity with. Marriage has a lot of ups and downs, and unconditional acceptance is a must. Christ never condoned sin, but he always accepted the sinner. We've been taught that a man should love his wife the way Christ loves his church. You're entitled to that. Maybe he'll come around. But if he doesn't, you'll find someone who will accept you. I'd bet on it."

An undeniable reality rushed out in fresh emotion. "I love him, Sean."

She was relieved when he didn't ask her to expound. He only put his arm around her and let her cry. Allison was actually beginning to feel better when the door opened. She discreetly dried her tears as Sariah walked in—with Ammon right behind her. What was bad suddenly became worse as she looked up to see his skeptical eyes taking in the way Sean had his arm around her.

Reminding herself that she had nothing to apologize for, she stood up, saying firmly, "Sean, you remember my roommate, Sariah, and this is her brother, Ammon."

Sean rose and shook their hands. "Hello, Sariah," he said warmly. "It's a pleasure to meet you, Ammon."

"This is Sean O'Hara," Allison said to Ammon, unable to deny something negative in his eyes.

"Good to see you again, Sean," Sariah said while Ammon scowled subtly toward Allison.

Sariah hurried to her room and Sean quickly said good-bye, pausing to kiss Allison's cheek and say, "You have a good Christmas, now. You know where I am if you need anything."

"Thank you," she said and squeezed his hand.

After Sean closed the door, Allison took a deep breath, cursing her heart for the way it reacted to having Ammon Mitchell in the room. She wanted to strangle Sariah for bringing him in like this and then abandoning her to be alone with him.

"This is an interesting little twist," Ammon said, as if he'd like to accuse her of committing fresh sin.

"He's married," she said, and Ammon's eyes widened. "I mean . . ." she stammered, realizing how that sounded, "he's like a brother to me, and . . ." Ammon's eyes widened impossibly further and Allison grimaced again, recalling her initial feelings for him. "You don't understand. My family took him in years ago. There was never anything romantic between us. My parents often ask him to check up on me. He's happily married. Is there anything else you want to know?"

Allison sensed he was gathering his thoughts to say something when Sariah erupted from her bedroom.

"Aren't you ready to go yet? Nana's going to wonder what happened to us."

"I . . . uh . . ." Allison stammered again, wishing Ammon would leave them with some privacy. Deciding she needed it whether he wanted to give it to her or not, she hurried to her room without explanation. She was glad Sariah picked up on the hint and followed her.

"I don't want to go, Sariah," she said as soon as the door was closed. "Tell your family I appreciate the invitation, but—"

"But nothing!" Sariah insisted. "What are you going to do? Sit here by yourself through the entire holiday? I don't think so. I won't let you. Now get your things together, and—"

"Sariah, listen to me. Things are not working out with me and Ammon. I'm not sure I can be in the same room with him while—"

"If you mean the little spat you had last night, I wouldn't be—"

"He told you?"

"Yes, he told me."

"Who else did he tell?"

"No one. He said you told him I already knew."

"And what did you say?" Allison asked.

"I told him he needed to buck up and act like a man."

"And?" Allison pressed.

"He's struggling with it. What difference does that make to spending Christmas with my family? He's just *one* of them. If he wants to be a jerk, let him. He told me it didn't make him care any less about you, it just—"

"Bothers him," Allison said with cynicism.

Sariah sighed. "Allison, this is between you and Ammon. What's between you and me is that you are supposed to spend Christmas with my family, and I'm not going to let my brother's bad attitude make you think you have to spend Christmas alone."

Allison sighed. She didn't *want* to spend Christmas by herself. She could probably go hang out at Sean's house, but she'd feel so out of place with his new little family. In lieu of not being able to go home, she'd truly been looking forward to this. If only she'd waited until after Christmas to tell Ammon! Oh, she'd made such a mess, and it all started years ago when she'd made some stupid mistakes.

"Come on, Allison," Sariah said. "Lupe loves you. She'll be so disappointed. I promise you won't have to be alone with Ammon for even a minute if you don't want to."

Allison sighed again, then nodded. "Okay, just give me a few minutes."

While Sariah went across the hall to gather her own things, Allison threw what she needed into an overnight bag, trying not to think about the reality that Ammon was waiting in the other room. She loaded the wrapped gifts into a shopping bag, grateful she'd not purchased anything terribly big or heavy.

"Need some help?" Ammon asked as she walked into the front room. Sariah was halfway out the door with her own things.

"Thanks, I've got it," she said, moving past him.

"I've checked the lights and turned the heat down," Sariah called back. "Go ahead and lock up."

Allison set a bag down to check the lock. Ammon picked up the bag and motioned her out the door. She scowled at him, wishing she had a clue what he was thinking. He smirked and said, "I can at least be your big brother, can't I?"

Allison hated the way that stung. Well, at least she didn't have to wonder. But after realizing how much she truly loved this man, accepting him as a brother figure wasn't going to be easy. She steeled herself to endure it for the next twenty-four hours, then she never had to see him again if she didn't want to.

Chapter Nine

Allison nudged Sariah into the truck first so she wouldn't have to sit next to Ammon. She didn't like the way the passenger seat felt unfamiliar after spending so many hours sitting next to him with her hand in his.

They arrived at Lupe's house to a mixture of aromas unlike anything Allison had ever experienced. Mosiah and Sally were sitting on the couch looking at a photo album. Helaman was dozing in a big chair.

"We're here!" Sariah called. Lupe and two other people—obviously Sariah's parents—hurried from the kitchen.

"Oh, there she is!" Lupe exclaimed, and Allison realized that all eyes were on her.

"Well, introduce us," Sariah's mother said. But she was talking to Ammon.

"Allison," he said, and she felt his hand briefly touch the small of her back, "these are my parents, Paul and Maria Mitchell. Mom, Dad, this is Allison."

While Allison was distracted by the heat generated from Ammon's touch, Maria stepped forward and took

Allison's face into her hands. "Oh, you sweet thing," she said, much like Lupe would have. "We've heard so many good things about you." Turning to Ammon, she added, "She's even more beautiful than you said she was."

Allison turned and briefly scowled at Ammon. He smiled, and she decided she'd give a lot to know where his thoughts were.

"It's a pleasure to meet you, young lady," Paul Mitchell said, stepping forward to shake her hand.

"And you," she practically squeaked. It was no wonder the Mitchell children were all so attractive. Their parents were beautiful people.

Allison was relieved when Sariah enlisted her help in wrapping some gifts, then setting the table for dinner. As the dinner hour came closer, the men hovered in the kitchen, snitching beans from the huge, simmering pot and eating them with tortillas heated over the gas flame on the stove. Lupe would slap their hands and tell them to wait. Then she would laugh, and it was evident she loved their impatience.

"You know what you need?" Ammon said to her. "You need a good dance."

"No," Lupe laughed, but Ammon pulled her close to him and urged her into an exaggerated waltz around the kitchen. Lupe giggled like a schoolgirl while the others clapped and cheered. Allison felt a twinge of envy at Lupe's being so close to Ammon.

"You haven't lost your touch, Nana," he said, setting her free to do her cooking.

When dinner was finally laid out, Allison felt as if she'd been transported to another place. As the tamales were served, Lupe explained, mostly to Allison, "It is said that we have tamales for Christmas in Mexico so that we'll have something to open."

Allison was warmed by the implication of humility. Sariah leaned over and whispered, "She's told us that at least a thousand times. She must appreciate having someone here who's never heard it before."

Allison enjoyed the meal. She never would have believed that rice and beans could taste so good. About halfway through the meal, Paul asked, "So Allison, what do you think of our traditional Christmas dinner?"

"It's wonderful," she said. "These are nothing like the tamales I've had. These are actually *good*."

Everyone chuckled and Sally said, "Just don't put ketchup on them. You'll insult Nana." Allison wondered if she was speaking from personal experience.

Ammon leaned toward Allison and said quietly, "It's a gringo thing."

"Nana cooked a ham once," Helaman said. "She wanted to give us an *American* Christmas dinner."

"Yes," Lupe waved her hand through the air, "and they all got angry with me; told me if I ever did it again, they'd disown me."

"What would Christmas be without tamales, Nana?" Mosiah asked.

"Well, we're having ham tomorrow," Lupe declared. "My sweet *viejo*; he loved his glazed ham."

Allison couldn't help noticing how Lupe became briefly distant, and tears rolled spontaneously down her cheeks. Allison whispered toward Sariah, who was at her right, "She really misses her husband, doesn't she?"

She was surprised to hear Ammon whisper from her left, "She believes she'll never see him again." Allison

turned to briefly meet his eyes, absorbing the implication. He added quietly, "She believes he's gone for
good."

Allison looked again at Lupe as she sighed and wiped
her tears away. She was tempted to cry herself as she
tried to comprehend how this woman must feel. She
wanted to ask if Lupe had been told about eternal
marriage and life after death. But Allison knew that she
had. With all these missionaries in Lupe's family, she'd
been told of such things repeatedly. But it was evident,
just as Sariah had told her, that Lupe had chosen to cling
to her own beliefs, in spite of the heartache that accom-
panied them. Allison said a quick prayer in her heart
that Lupe would one day accept the truth and be
reunited with her sweet *viejo*. She tried to comprehend
the love this woman had for her husband, and without
thinking, her gaze turned to Ammon. He caught her
watching him and she looked abruptly away, nearly
wishing she'd never met him.

Allison discreetly observed those around her and
quickly surmised that the rice and beans were meant to
be eaten together—literally. This was confirmed when
Lupe ended up with a small serving of rice on her plate,
barely two or three bites. She said earnestly, "Will
someone pass the beans so that I can finish my rice?"

Allison observed the simple ritual and felt warmed.
She had truly come to love these people—all of them.
She reminded herself that she could still be close to the
family, whether or not Ammon wanted anything to do
with her.

While the table was being cleared, Allison slipped
away to the bathroom. She came out to find Ammon

waiting in the hall. Caught briefly off guard, she quickly motioned toward the bathroom door, saying, "It's all yours."

His expression told her he hadn't been waiting for the bathroom. This set Allison's nerves on edge, but she managed to keep a straight face.

"Are you okay?" he asked gently.

"I'd rather not get into it now," she insisted and hurried back to the kitchen. In her present state of mind, she feared that *any* conversation with Ammon Mitchell would reduce her to tears.

After dinner was cleaned up, the family gathered around the Christmas tree. Candles were lit, and the nativity was read in a way Allison had never heard before as members of the family each took certain parts. It was something like a simplified readers' theater. Allison felt the Spirit close to her as she absorbed the beauty of the tree, covered with an array of ornaments, many that were nearly as old as Lupe. The flames of many candles reflected off the faces of these people she'd come to care for, and in spite of her present heartache, she couldn't deny her gratitude for having this experience.

Later in the evening, Allison enjoyed watching the family members each open a gift from their parents. They were all histrionically pretending to be surprised to receive plaid flannel pajamas. It became evident to Allison that getting new pajamas on Christmas Eve was a tradition that had not wavered as the children had become adults. Maria had made all the pajamas, and she declared that everyone usually wore them all day on Christmas. Allison was feeling an ache for her own home and family when Maria plopped a package onto her lap.

"Open it," Sariah said with a little laugh.

Allison was so surprised she could hardly speak when she realized that she'd been given a pair of pajamas, too.

"Sariah told me the two of you were about the same size," Maria said with a smile.

"Thank you," Allison said. "I don't know what to say."

"Think nothing of it," Paul insisted. "You're practically one of the family." Allison felt a little uneasy at this, but a quick glance at Ammon showed his indifference. They were obviously referring to her friendship with Sariah.

Allison's next surprise was the realization that everyone but Sariah's parents and Lupe would be sleeping on the family room floor in the basement.

"It's a tradition," Sariah said as sleeping bags were being dragged out and furniture was pushed aside. "Ever since we were little kids, we'd always sleep together downstairs—whether we were home or at Nana's."

"It's not because we loved each other," Helaman interjected, decked out in his new—thankfully, very modest—pajamas. "It's because we didn't trust each other."

His brothers laughed and Sally added, "You still don't trust each other."

Mosiah added, "We don't want anybody sneaking upstairs on their own to see if Santa has come."

When everybody was ready for bed, and Allison was trying hard to remain inconspicuous and keep her distance from Ammon, they all gathered on the floor to play *Uno*. Allison nearly forgot about the tension she was feeling as the game became hysterical. Paul, Maria, and Lupe came down the stairs to see what was going on. Allison had to admit it was a humorous picture: six adults wearing matching pajamas, laughing ridiculously loud, eating popcorn, with sleeping bags haphazardly spread across the floor around them.

"You haven't done your song," Sariah said to her brothers while their parents and Lupe were in the room. The men laughed and protested until the others pleaded and begged them to do *their song*, whatever it might be.

Allison wondered if she had ever laughed so hard in her life as Mosiah, Helaman, and Ammon stood close together and sang a comical version, with their own lyrics, of *We Three Kings*. When it was finished, they all bowed ridiculously while the family applauded. Sariah leaned over to Allison and said, "They made that up when I was about eight. They've been doing it ever since."

As they settled back into their game, Allison again found her mind preoccupied with what a wonderful family this was. Then a little heartache crept in as she thought of the chance she'd lost to be a part of it. Her mind wandered to Ammon, to the strength of her feelings, and she wondered why it had to be this way. Almost against her will, she found herself watching him. She became absorbed with the way he could make her heart quicken. It was ironic that he had taught her to learn to rely on others more, had shown her that she couldn't make it through this life alone. But now she had to accept the possibility of making it without him. It took her a moment to realize that he was watching her, too. He smiled as if nothing in the world was wrong. She felt certain he was trying to let her know that they could still be friends. But the reality made her

115

"It's there," Lupe motioned toward the stove where a kettle of water was steaming, and the can of cocoa mix sat close by. Allison found herself a cup and spoon.

"Sit down with me, Allison. I feel as if I know you so well from the things the children have told me. But you and I haven't had a chance to talk much."

"There's always something going on, it seems," Allison said, slowly stirring her cocoa.

"Yes," Lupe smiled, "and then it's so quiet when they're not here."

She sighed and Allison said, "You love your family very much."

"Yes," she smiled, "they are so good to me."

"Obviously because you have been good to them."

"I would like to think so. Of course, it used to be that many more were here. I have seven children, you know. Two have passed on, but their children are many. Most of them live too far away to visit for holidays. Many of them write and call; I'm glad for that. Some don't seem to take an interest in staying close to old Nana."

Allison impulsively took the older woman's hand across the table. "They don't know what they're missing. I've enjoyed every minute in your home."

Lupe smiled widely, and Allison could see in her a vague resemblance to Ammon. "And you will be spending much more time in my home, I hear."

Allison glanced down quickly. When things had erupted between her and Ammon, she hadn't taken into account the fact that he had already shared his feelings with his family, and that all of this would affect them, as well.

"Is something wrong, child?" Lupe asked. Allison didn't know how to answer. While she was still contemplating it, Lupe added, "Is there trouble between you and Ammon . . . already?"

Allison sighed. "I fear there is. It would seem we have some differences that I'm not certain can be overcome."

Lupe looked concerned. "Well, I'm not going to pry. It's none of my business what those differences might be. But I know that when two people truly care for each other, there's nothing that can't be overcome with some effort."

Allison sighed and looked down. She didn't want to admit that at the moment she found such a concept difficult to believe. Ammon's words of nonacceptance were still stinging.

"Have you talked to him about it?" Lupe asked gently. "Have you told him the truth of what's in your heart?"

Allison looked into Lupe's wise countenance. "Only when we were both angry."

Lupe made a noise of disgust. "That's not talking. You mustn't let go of it without knowing that you've shared your whole heart with him, child. Promise me that."

Allison hesitated, then nodded.

Lupe added, "And if he's listened to anything I've taught him, you can bet that he'll be doing the same."

Allison thought of his attempts to talk to her last night, and the way she'd walked away or ignored him. But then, in the same house with his entire family, with celebrations taking place, was neither the time nor the place. A part of her couldn't help hoping they could come to terms with this, but a bigger part of her was skeptical. Had she just been hurt too many times to believe it could really work out? Or was there something deeper? She wondered in moments like this if the difficult relationship she'd observed between her parents as a child had affected her more than she realized. She wondered if she was being stubborn and presumptuous, and resigned herself to at least talk to Ammon—tomorrow, when Christmas was over. For now, she just had to endure his presence and enjoy the day ahead.

She was startled from her thoughts when Lupe added gently, "You mustn't worry, my darling girl. Things that are meant to be have a way of working themselves out."

Allison smiled, wanting with everything inside to believe her. As she looked into the old woman's eyes, a thought occurred to her that she felt compelled to share.

"You know, Lupe," Allison said, taking her hand across the table, "I want to share something with you, and I hope that you won't be offended. I don't claim to understand your beliefs, and I know they're a big part of your upbringing. I just want to tell you . . . I know with all my heart . . ." Allison wasn't prepared for the tears that burned into her eyes, as if to confirm the truth of what she was saying, ". . . that you will be with your husband again. The love you share with him will be eternal. Your children will see to that, I'm certain."

While Allison watched Lupe's inquisitive gaze, and the tears that brimmed in her big, dark eyes, she added gently, "You just said yourself that when something is meant to be, it has a way of working itself out."

Lupe smiled serenely. "So I did."

Allison didn't know if her brief testimony would leave any impression, but she felt certain that whether it happened in this life or the next, Lupe would eventually be able to accept the truth of the gospel and its promises of eternity. She knew that this dear woman would be with her beautiful family forever—and she tried to ignore the twinge of heartache she felt in wishing that she, too, could be a part of that family.

Chapter Ten

The timer on the stove rang, and Lupe rose to take something out of the oven.

"It smells wonderful," Allison said.

"*Pan dulce*," Lupe said. At Allison's questioning gaze she interpreted, "Sweet bread. We'll have it to tide us over, and then we'll all fix a big brunch together. That's the way we've always done it."

Allison smiled, and a moment later the others began filtering into the kitchen, as if the smell of freshly baked Mexican sweet bread had interrupted their dreams and urged them here. Allison's heart quickened at the sight of Ammon, his hair mussed from sleep, a dark shadow showing on his face. He smiled at her, and she thought that she should at least talk to him.

"She's a traitor," Helaman exclaimed facetiously, pointing at Allison. "She abandoned us all and came up here alone to scout out the goods."

Lupe laughed and pointed a scolding finger at him. "I can assure you she's been sitting right here with me. She's not had a peek at whatever Santa might have brought . . . as if he'd bring anything for a bunch of overgrown children like the lot of you."

They all laughed and dug into the warm *pan dulce*, then the day became like a whirlwind. First there was the gift-opening frenzy. Allison was grateful for her prompting to buy gifts for everyone when she was showered with more gifts than she could have imagined. They were small and inexpensive, but the thoughtfulness touched her— that a family she barely knew would take her in and see that she had a good Christmas, knowing her own family was so far away. Then she thought of the way her parents had taken Sean in and treated him like one of their own. She found it intriguing how blessings had a way of coming back around. Her parents certainly deserved to know that their daughter was being looked out for.

When Ammon opened the gifts from her, she thought for a moment that he was going to cry. But he only smiled at her with eyes that seemed full of love and acceptance. She had to admit that she was grateful he had no animosity toward her, even if marriage was not an option under the circumstances.

Allison felt a little nervous opening the three gifts that Ammon had given her. The first was a beautiful pair of gloves. Trying them on brought back memories of their sleigh ride. She thought it funny that they'd given each other the same thing. The next gift surprised her even more.

"What is it?" Sariah insisted while she just stared into the box.

Allison pulled it out. "It's a Mickey Mouse watch." She couldn't resist looking straight at Ammon as she asked, "How did you know?"

"That you needed a watch? It was a little obvious."

"I know that," she laughed softly. "I mean . . . my mother has always worn a Mickey Mouse watch . . . for as long as I can remember."

Ammon smiled and sent her heart fluttering. "Just a lucky guess, I suppose," he said, with something almost sad in his voice. Did he feel the same irony she did? Was it enough to soften his heart toward her mistakes?

She told herself not to get her hopes up, and simply smiled toward him. "Thank you, Ammon," she said. "I love it."

"One more," he said and handed her a big, square box. She laughed when she opened it and found a basketball. "For one-on-one," he said with a little smirk. Allison just thanked him and resisted the urge to cry.

When the gifts had been opened, everyone pitched in to make a big brunch. They had a cleanup project, then began a round of games while everyone—even Paul, Maria, and Lupe—remained in their pajamas. They played *Charades*, *Pictionary*, and some role-playing games that Allison found fascinating. At one point, when they were supposed to pair off, Helaman went with his sister, and that left Allison and Ammon sitting next to each other on the couch. Allison's heart nearly beat through her chest when he took her hand and squeezed it affectionately. Their eyes met for a moment as she attempted to question his motives. He only smiled and turned his attention to the game.

The final game was the breaking of the piñata. While they were taking turns swinging at it, Maria declared, "You people need to get busy and get us some grandchildren. You're all getting much too big for this, but we can't have Christmas without a piñata."

125

"We're working on it," Mosiah said, rubbing Sally's belly that was still flat and firm.

"What's wrong with the rest of you?" Paul said with a comical scowl at his other children. Allison felt herself turn warm, although he didn't even glance at her.

They all finally got dressed for Christmas dinner. Allison actually felt choked up when the family gathered around the huge table, beautifully spread with a glazed ham and all the traditional trimmings, along with a touch of Mexico.

She felt the urge to cry again as Paul gave a beautiful prayer over the meal, expressing gratitude for the Savior's birth, as well as the life he lived. She wondered briefly what Lupe thought of the LDS beliefs shared by this branch of her posterity. Observing, it seemed that they all believed in the same God, and for Lupe, that was good enough. Allison hoped the things she had said earlier this morning would at least give Lupe a glimmer of hope that she could be with her beloved husband again. There was some comfort in knowing that people like Lupe would have another chance in the next life to accept the truth. Just as she'd told Lupe this morning, she felt certain that eventually Lupe would be with her sweet *viejo*.

In spite of somehow ending up right next to Ammon at the table, Allison again wondered if she had ever enjoyed a meal so much. Everyone seemed to have all the time in the world. They ate slowly, laughing and talking of memories and dreams. Allison thought how wonderful it was that adult siblings could have so much love and camaraderie among them. She had several refills of the red fruit punch they were drinking, wondering why it tasted so good. Maybe it was the beautiful stemmed glassware that chimed from the ice cubes dancing in it. Maybe it was the atmosphere. Maybe it was the company.

When the meal was finished but everyone hovered at the table, Allison felt a little uncomfortable. They all seemed to be waiting for something to happen, and she seemed to be the only one who didn't know what it was. They continued to converse nonchalantly, but that feeling of anticipation only intensified. She just sipped her punch and listened, enjoying their banter, mingling it with thoughts of home. Occasionally she caught Ammon's eye, wondering over the apparent sparkle she saw there. Perhaps there was hope yet, she thought. Perhaps with time he would come to see that her mistakes were in the past, and he would be willing to share a future with her.

As Allison finished off her punch and glanced at what was left of the ice cubes clinging to the bottom of her glass, she noticed something unusual. She nearly went cross-eyed as she attempted to focus on it. At first she thought it was just a trick of the light, but looking closer, she realized there was something frozen into one of the ice cubes. She wondered if this was some family tradition. Is that what they were all waiting for, to see who got the prize in their drink? Trying to be discreet and not draw attention to herself, Allison tipped her glass and carefully peered into it. Suddenly she found it difficult to breathe. While she was trying to convince herself that it wasn't her imagination, she heard Ammon say in a voice that startled her, "Is something wrong, Allison?"

"What?" she glanced up, feeling like she'd been caught at mischief. It only took a moment to absorb his satisfied smile and to glance around the table and realize that everyone else had a similar expression. Ammon chuckled and she turned back to look at him, trying to figure what was happening.

"Is something wrong?" Ammon repeated.

Convincing herself it was some kind of game, she just said, "There's . . . something in my drink."

"It's not alive, I hope," Helaman said.

Allison looked into her glass again, and suddenly felt as frozen as the little pieces of ice she was looking at. She didn't know what to say or do without making an utter fool of herself. The evidence before her eyes simply didn't mesh with what she believed.

"Let me see that," Ammon said, taking the glass from her. He looked into it, saying with no expression, "Sure enough. There's something in there."

"Is this some kind of game?" Allison found the voice to ask.

"No," Sariah chuckled from across the table, "it's not a game."

"It's a joke, then, right?" she asked, her embarrassment rising from being the obvious center of attention. The family was looking at her as if she'd just been announced as the new Miss America.

Ammon reached two fingers into her glass and pulled out what was left of the responsible ice cube, setting it in his palm. "It's no joke," he said, holding it close to Allison's face. "It looks like a ring to me."

Allison sucked in her breath. Was he trying to say what seemed obvious? She hardly dared hope. Their eyes met and she felt him press the piece of ice into her hand, wrapping her fingers tightly around it. She could feel it turning to water from the heat of her skin as Ammon added, "When it melts you can try it on . . . if you'll have me."

Allison pressed her other hand over her mouth as emotion threatened to overwhelm her. She was still trying to convince herself that this was what it seemed to be when Paul bellowed lightly, "Do it right, boy, or I'll box your ears."

"You know," Mosiah said, "he's been threatening that for years. I've still never seen him box anybody's ears."

"Just keep it up," Paul added with a chuckle.

Allison felt herself losing control as Ammon abruptly pushed back his chair and went down on one knee, taking her hand into his, apparently oblivious to the water dripping between her fingers from the melting ice.

"Allison," he said with a fervency in his voice that pushed her emotions to a breaking point, "I love you. I love you for who you are, for everything that has made you who you are. I want to be with you forever." He paused and smiled, while Allison kept her other hand pressed tightly to her mouth. "Will you marry me, Allison?"

That did it. Allison had no choice but to break into uncontrollable tears or pass out. She was oblivious to anything but the pure, perfect joy surging through every nerve as she cried helplessly. She was vaguely aware of Ammon chuckling warmly near her ear as he pulled her to his shoulder and held her tight. She didn't know how long she cried before it came back to her that she was being observed by the entire family. She glanced up and pressed a hand over her eyes as the embarrassment took hold. Gradually her tears turned to a laughter that deepened when Ammon said, "Can I take that as a *yes*?"

Allison tried with everything she had to say something, but all she could do was hover back and forth between laughter and tears. She watched him unfold her fingers, where the ring was lying in her wet palm. He carefully picked it up and slid it onto her third finger, provoking a fresh bout of tears.

"I love you," she finally managed, pushing her arms around his shoulders. Ammon sat on his chair and urged Allison onto his lap, holding her close. When she finally calmed down enough to wipe the tears off her face, she said, "I've never been so embarrassed in my life."

A variety of chuckles eased the tension, then Allison realized she wasn't the only one in the room who was sniffling. A moment later, Lupe said, "I think that is the sweetest thing I have ever seen in my whole life."

Now that the spectacle was over, the family began leaving the table and clearing it. Ammon took Allison's hand and led her to the front room, where only the Christmas tree lights were on. He sat on the couch and urged her close to him, putting his arm around her. He pressed a kiss into her hair, saying quietly, "There's something I need to ask you, Allison."

"Okay," she said and sniffled.

"I need to ask your forgiveness," he whispered. She looked up in surprise to find his eyes moist with emotion. "It didn't take me long to realize what a fool I'd made of myself. I just didn't know how to let you know without putting my foot further into my mouth. When I told Sariah what an idiot I'd been, she agreed." He laughed softly and eased her a little closer. "She

130

suggested that I just ask you to marry me and get it over with. I wanted to let you know what I was thinking, and warn you somehow, but honestly, I just didn't get a chance. We never had a moment alone."

Allison laughed softly, thinking of how hard she had tried to avoid being alone with him.

"Anyway," he went on, "I didn't sleep at all the night we talked. I admit that it bothered me, but as I prayed to understand and come to terms with it, I realized *why* it bothered me. It wasn't because I believed I was somehow better than you or something; I hope you understand that. I think I was . . . *jealous*. I want you to know that I admire you, Allison, for rising above it to go on a mission. I love you for the testimony you have, among other things. I won't question whatever personal hell you went through to get it. Sariah, bless her heart, reminded me of some things that made me take a good, long look at the situation. She said that in today's world, immorality struggles are likely in epidemic proportions. It's a tough time to live in, and I know Satan puts in overtime with Mormon kids. The likelihood of marrying someone who hasn't struggled with such things to some degree is pretty minimal. The important thing is how a person deals with their mistakes, and you are a perfect example of how to do it right."

Allison started to cry again, but she didn't feel embarrassed as Ammon eased her closer. "Merry Christmas, Allison. Today we celebrate, not only the birth of our Savior, but his life . . . and his death, and what it means to us as individuals. He's covered your mistakes, Allison. And he's covered mine. And that's really what Christmas is all about."

Chapter Eleven

Once the Christmas celebrations were finished, Allison and Ammon talked far into the night about the issue that had briefly come between them. Allison felt completely at peace to know that Ammon's acceptance was genuine. He understood the feelings behind her rebellion and the things she had learned.

Even though it was late, Allison called her parents as soon as Ammon took her back to the apartment. It was difficult to separate herself from him, but there was peace in knowing that everything was as it should be between them. She had stumbled upon her destiny, and she knew it with every fiber of her being.

With the time difference between Australia and Utah, Allison was able to talk to each member of the family. She had to bite her tongue to keep from blurting out the news. She wanted to surprise them, and hoped her plan would work.

"Mom, Dad," she said, knowing they were each on an extension, "there's so much I want to tell you . . . about what I did for Christmas. Sariah's family is so incredible."

Emily laughed through the phone. "You sound as if you really enjoyed it."

"Oh, I did . . . but, well . . . since I don't have a job at the moment, I have nothing to do until classes start again after the new year. I want to come home. Would that be all right?"

Allison couldn't tell if they were laughing or crying. Michael finally said, "Oh, it would be more than all right, sweetie. You go ahead and charge a ticket to my credit card. I know you have the number."

"That would be great, Dad . . . but since I spent Christmas with a friend, would it be all right if I bring a friend home with me? Do you think you can afford it?"

Michael laughed. "It would be a pleasure."

"Thanks, Dad. You're the greatest. I love you . . . both of you. I can't wait to see you."

"The same here," Emily said. "We'll be counting the hours. And I think we'll just have to have Christmas dinner all over again when you come."

"That sounds great."

Michael called the next morning to be certain that she'd been able to make flight arrangements. She told him she hadn't had any trouble. It seemed now that Christmas was over, you could get just about anywhere pretty easily. As soon as she hung up with her father, she called Ammon.

"Hi," she said as soon as he answered.

"Well, hello the future Mrs. Mitchell," he replied with so much warmth in his voice that Allison had trouble speaking. "What's up?" he asked, startling her back to the moment.

"Well," she said, "it looks like you're going to get to meet my parents."

"Are they coming here?" he asked with obvious pleasure.

"No, we're going there."

"*Australia?*" he squeaked.

"It's my hometown."

"Wow," he laughed. "How did you pull that off?"

Allison told him her plan and how her father had eagerly paid for the tickets. She laughed as she told him that they would likely assume she was bringing Sariah home with her.

"Don't tell her," Ammon said. "My sister will be furious with me if she finds out she missed a trip to Australia."

"Actually, I already told her," Allison admitted. "I think she's so excited that I'm going to be her sister-in-law, she really doesn't care."

"Well, she's not the only one who's excited," Ammon said, then they laughed together from the pure happiness they shared.

The following day, Ammon picked Allison up just after lunch and loaded her luggage into the back of the truck. They wandered around Salt Lake City for a while and had dinner, then they ambled through Temple Square, marveling at the Christmas lights that seemed so magical. Before leaving for the airport, they stood for a long while observing the nativity on the lawn, and the view of the Christus statue in the distance through the glass wall of the Visitors' Center.

"It's so beautiful," Allison said, nuzzling closer to Ammon's warmth as the wind increased.

"Yes it is," he agreed. Their eyes met and he admitted, "I've never been so happy in my life."

"You and me both," she replied and he kissed her, making her oblivious to the surrounding cold.

On the flight from Salt Lake City to Los Angeles, they discussed a possible date to be married. Comparing their planners, they tentatively decided on the first weekend in March, in the Salt Lake Temple.

"That's a long way for your family to travel," Ammon said. "Isn't the bride supposed to get married in her hometown?"

"Well, I was born in Utah, and I've lived here for many years, on and off. My family can afford to come here, and then you and I will go there for an open house. How does that sound?"

"Marvelous," he said. "Maybe an Australian honeymoon would fit nicely in between."

Allison laughed, unable to hold back her joy.

On the flight from L.A. to Sydney, they mostly slept. As they landed, Allison noticed that Ammon seemed a little nervous.

"Is something wrong?" she asked.

"I just realized that I'm meeting my future in-laws. What if they don't like me? What if—"

"Don't be ridiculous. They'll love you." She kissed him and added, "How could they not?"

"I guess we'll see," he said and took a deep breath as the plane halted at the gate.

While they were gathering their things, Allison explained, "We have to take another flight to get home, but it will be on a private plane."

"Really? Who's flying it?"

"My father. They'll be here to meet us," she added as they stepped off the plane. "Just be cool and try to make the surprise good."

Ammon hung back discreetly as Allison embraced

her parents, laughing with more happiness than she believed she'd ever felt.

"Mom, Dad," she said as they glanced around for this friend she was supposed to be bringing, "I want you to know that I figured out why I couldn't come home for Christmas."

"And why is that?" Michael asked.

"Because of your grandmother's funeral?" Emily added.

"Well, I needed to be there for the funeral, yes—and I need to tell you about that. I think you'll appreciate some things that happened. But I still could have made it home for Christmas if I'd wanted to badly enough, I think."

"Then, why?" Emily asked.

Allison discreetly motioned Ammon forward as she held out her left hand toward her parents. "I needed to be in Utah so that I could get this."

Emily took Allison's hand and gasped. Her eyes widened with unspoken questions as she absorbed the fact that her daughter was wearing an engagement ring.

"Are you trying to tell us that . . ." Michael began but didn't finish. Allison felt their eyes move toward Ammon as they both seemed to realize that Allison wasn't alone after all.

"Mom, Dad," she said, taking Ammon's hand, "meet my fiancé, Ammon Mitchell."

A surprised little laugh erupted from Michael's lips, while Emily seemed unable to make any sound at all. After a long, tense moment, Michael reached out to take Ammon's hand, shaking it firmly. "It's a pleasure, young man. Welcome to Australia."

"Thank you, sir," he said congenially, but Allison could tell he was nervous.

Allison was momentarily speechless. Initially, she had difficulty absorbing the fact that someone as incredible as Ammon Mitchell had ever been subject to prejudice in his lifetime. She recalled now that Sariah had shared a few incidents from her childhood where she had been excluded or teased because of her appearance. The look in Ammon's eyes made it evident that the diversity of culture in his background had been a two-edged sword. She was quick to assure him, "My mother is not that way, Ammon. I've never seen even a hint of prejudice in her. We have many employees who are aborigines, and she's always—"

"But none of them ever came home and announced that they were going to marry her daughter." He sighed, and his eyes turned distant. "She's facing the reality that her grandchildren are not going to look like they belong to her."

Allison was tempted to defend her mother again, but a part of her had to wonder if he was right. She attempted to turn her concern to compassion on his behalf. Touching his face, she said, "I get the impression that this has come up before."

Ammon took a deep breath. "I told you about Carolyn, the woman I almost married." Allison nodded. "Well, she had some relatives who were absolutely appalled that she wasn't marrying a Caucasian. She had a fairly good attitude about it, but when other differences came up, I didn't believe we had the strength to stand up against that prejudice for the rest of our lives. I didn't want my children feeling like they were outcasts at every family gathering, or—"

"Ammon," she interrupted, "my mother is not a prejudiced person."

"Okay," he said, "then maybe you'd better talk to her and find out what's wrong." Allison nodded and he took her hand. "What if she is, Allison? What if she wants you to marry a white man?"

Allison didn't hesitate even a moment. "She'll just have to live with it. You and I are meant to be together. I know that with all my heart." She kissed him and added, "And our children are going to be *beautiful.*"

Ammon laughed softly and held her close. "I love you," he whispered, and Allison knew he meant it.

When Michael came out to see how they were doing, it was the perfect opportunity to leave Ammon in his care and seek out her mother. Allison found Emily in her sitting room, dabbing oils onto a canvas while she looked at an enlarged photograph of the farmhouse she'd grown up in.

"It's beautiful," Allison observed.

"Well," Emily said, "it's coming along. We'll see how it turns out before we make any conclusions." She looked past Allison and asked, "Where is Ammon?"

"He's with Dad." Allison hesitated and asked, "Can we talk?"

"Of course," Emily said, but there was something hesitant in her response.

"Mother," Allison said, sitting down in a chair nearby, "you always taught me to be straightforward and not let feelings go unsaid. Well, I'm getting the impression that there is something you're not saying." Emily stopped painting, but she didn't move. "Mother, is there a reason you're not happy about my engagement?"

While Allison had hoped that Emily would immediately assure her the assumption was wrong, her heart quickened at Emily's concerned gaze. She set down her brush and turned on her stool, sighing in a way that made it evident she didn't want to talk about this.

While Allison was wondering what else to say to get this out in the open—whatever it was—Michael came into the room.

"Where's Ammon?" she asked.

"He's with your sisters in the stables. I think they'll keep him occupied." He leaned against the door and added, "Do you want me to leave, or—"

"No," Emily said and held out her hand toward him. They moved to a little sofa across from Allison. Emily finally said, "Allison, Ammon is obviously a wonderful man. It's just that . . ."

"What, Mother?" Allison pressed when she didn't go on.

"I'm just concerned, sweetie. This happened so fast. At Thanksgiving, you didn't even know the man. It's not yet New Year's Day. How can you possibly know that—"

"I *know*, Mother. This is the right thing to do. I just feel it."

"Yes, well . . ." Emily's voice turned faintly sour, "I felt like I was supposed to marry your father, but it didn't necessarily turn out well."

"Is that what this is about?" Allison asked. "You're concerned that my marriage will turn out like yours did?"

Emily said nothing.

"Do you think I didn't see what you went through? I remember how he treated you. *You're* the one who taught me to be assertive, to define myself righteously, to treat myself as a daughter of God and insist on that treatment from others."

"Yes, Allison, but your childhood was still marred by emotional abuse in the home. It was not necessarily severe, but it was there."

"Yes, I know it was there. And that's why I'm not going to let it happen in my home. Ammon is a good man. His family is the best, and—"

"Yes, well," Emily retorted, "that's exactly what I thought about your father and *his* family. You know as well as I do that there were a lot of problems there that might not have been immediately evident; problems that affected me and my children."

"I'm not going to live like that, Mother," Allison insisted. "Even *if* Ammon had problems, I would not allow such things to go on in my home."

"That's a nice thought, Allison. But that's what most people who were beaten as children say. And then they end up beating their own children. It's subconscious, and I fear that it's—"

"Excuse me," Michael said, "but there's something you're overlooking." With his eyes fixed on Emily, he said, "You told me beyond any doubt that you were meant to marry Ryan; that it was what the Lord wanted you to do. And in the long run, we were all blessed because of it. Life is a struggle. There's no way around it. I was under the impression, Emily my dear, that you believed it was important to do what the Lord wanted, then take it on and learn from it. You fasted and prayed about marrying Ryan."

Emily turned to Allison and sighed. "Have you fasted and prayed about this, Allie?"

"No, but if you want me to, I will. It won't change anything. I've learned to recognize the Spirit's approval,

Mother, and there is no question that I have it in this marriage."

"But, maybe you should—" Emily began, but Michael interrupted.

"Emily, did you fast and pray about marrying me?" She scowled at him and he added, "You told me you didn't need to; that you knew it was right. You and I dated a long time in college, Emily, but it took about ten minutes for me to know that you and I were meant to be together. For some it might not be that way, but it was for me. We've done our best to teach Allison what's right and to take good care of herself and those she loves. She has a strong testimony and a lot of experience behind her. Now it's up to us to let her make her choices and support her in them unconditionally. Ammon's a good man," he finished.

"I know he is," Emily said tearfully, finding refuge on Michael's shoulder. Allison met her father's eyes while Emily cried. She finally added, "I just want you to be happy, Allison. I just think how blindly I walked into marriage, believing that everything would be good just because we were married in the temple. Marriage takes hard work."

"I know, Mother. I've also spent many years observing your marriage to Michael. Do you think I haven't noticed how much the two of you love each other, in spite of the struggles? And I also noticed how much you've always loved *me*—in spite of some big mistakes."

Following a long silence, Emily asked, "Does Ammon know about that?"

Warmth filled Allison from the inside out as she answered with confidence. "Yes, he does. He loves me. I love him. We know we're meant to be together."

146

Emily sighed. "I can't dispute that, Allison. Forgive me for my hesitance. I was just . . . caught by surprise, I suppose. And with your grandmother just passing away and all, I think my mind has been preoccupied with some of the struggles."

Allison took the opportunity to share with her parents the conversations she'd had with her grandmother, and the letter she had received through Louise on the day of the funeral. Allison sensed the healing in her mother as the many years of tension between her and her first mother-in-law were now laid to rest. Emily admitted that she was grateful for Allison listening to the Spirit and taking the time to go to the funeral.

When the conversation ran down, Emily reached out and took Allison's hand. "I'm truly happy for you, Allison. Ammon is obviously a wonderful man."

"I think you'd better tell *him* that," Allison said and Emily's alarm was evident.

"Does he think—"

"He's concerned that for some reason you don't like him, or don't approve of . . ."

"Of what?" Michael questioned when she hesitated.

"Well, apparently he's been a victim of prejudice before. He just needs to know that my family accepts him."

Michael hurried toward the door with Emily's hand in his. "I think we'd better straighten this out right now, darlin'."

Allison followed after her parents, relieved to have their approval. They found Ammon sitting on a corral fence, looking thoughtful.

"Where did everyone go?" Allison asked as they approached.

Ammon turned and jumped down. She sensed his nervousness at seeing her parents coming close behind her. "They went riding. They invited me along, but I told them I'd wait for you."

While Allison was wondering how to approach this, Emily pushed past her and took both of Ammon's hands into hers.

"Allison and I have been talking. I'll let her tell you what was said later on. But I want to make one thing perfectly clear, Ammon. My concerns have nothing to do with you personally. Maybe I'm just not wanting my daughter to grow up. But she's a woman now, and she's proven many times over to have a strong spirit and good instincts. We're pleased and happy to have you a part of our family."

"Thank you," Ammon said with a little laugh of relief.

"She just doesn't want to be old enough to be a grandmother," Michael teased.

Emily retorted, "I just don't want to have to sleep with a grandfather."

Michael laughed and hugged his wife.

"We're not even married yet," Allison insisted, putting her arm around Ammon.

"Well, when the time comes," Emily said, "we're certainly going to have beautiful grandchildren." She added in a dramatic whisper toward her daughter, "That alone makes him an ideal catch."

Ammon hugged Allison tightly, then they walked back to the house to discuss plans for the wedding. After everyone had gone to bed, Allison and Ammon sat by the Christmas tree, planning their future and sharing their dreams. Then they sat in comfortable silence until Ammon pressed his lips into Allison's hair.

"Merry Christmas," he whispered. "I feel as if I've finally come home."

Allison absorbed the warm spirit surrounding them and silently agreed. With Ammon, anywhere could be home.

$\mathcal{C}hapter\ \mathcal{T}welve$

One Year Later

"This is absolutely ridiculous," Allison snarled. "It's Christmas Eve, and we're *here*."

"Yes, we are," Ammon replied matter-of-factly, gazing out the window at the heavy snowfall being thrashed about on gusts of wind. The television, turned low, was playing the musical version of *A Christmas Carol.*

"We should be at your grandmother's right now," Allison continued with chagrin in her voice. "We should be eating tamales and beans and—"

"You would probably get heartburn," Ammon replied coolly. He turned from the view of the storm and sat down beside Allison, taking her hand into his.

Allison ignored him and continued her tirade. "We should be wearing matching flannel pajamas and sleeping on the family room floor with the rest of your family. But *no*," she drawled with sarcasm. "We had to be *here*."

Ammon chuckled, and she turned to him with a scowl. "What are you laughing about? This is not funny!"

"That is a matter of opinion, Mrs. Mitchell. In my *opinion*, this is an ideal way to spend Christmas."

Allison looked appalled and he laughed. "How do you figure?" she asked. "This is not exactly what I had in mind to do with my holiday season."

"So, life threw us a little curve ball." He pressed a kiss to her brow. "But I think we'll find a lot of silver linings in this cloud."

"Eventually . . . but right now, I'd rather be—"

Ammon kissed her to stop the protests. "Allison, my love," he said gently, "it doesn't matter where you want to be right now, we are here, and there's nothing anyone can do about it." He pressed a kiss to her brow and pushed her hair back with his fingers. "Like I said before, I think this is an ideal way to spend Christmas Eve."

"How do you figure?" she asked again, although more softly.

"Because," he said, pressing a hand over her rounded belly, "this is how Mary spent Christmas Eve . . . in a manner of speaking."

Allison marveled freshly at what a good man she had married. He always managed to find the good in everything, and he loved her even when she complained. Being numb from the waist down, she felt little evidence that she was in labor. While Ammon sat close beside her, watching her more than the movie, her mind tallied all that had happened in a year.

Ammon's work as a contractor was going well. He provided a good living for them, and he had built them a beautiful home. Allison had managed to get in several college credits and work a part-time job up until her seventh month. Of course, neither of them had expected a baby so soon, but they had both concluded that under the circumstances, this child must have a good reason for coming now.

Still, it wasn't due for nearly two weeks, and going into labor the morning of Christmas Eve had thrown off their plans for the holiday. Allison wasn't very happy about it, but Ammon seemed to have a gift of helping her see the good in life. As her labor progressed, Allison thought more and more about what he'd said. She tried to imagine Mary giving birth in a stable. She wouldn't have had any anesthetic, or clean sheets beneath her, or the evidence of medical technology to be certain that nothing would go wrong.

Allison was nearly dozing when Ammon nudged her with the phone. "It's your parents. I finally got through."

"Is it true?" Emily asked. "You're really in labor?"

"I really am," Allison replied.

"I'm not old enough to be a grandfather," Michael insisted from the extension.

"Come to Utah and I'll prove otherwise," Allison said.

"Well, we're going to do just that." Emily's voice betrayed her excitement. "As soon as we got the message, we made reservations. We'll be on our way almost as soon as Christmas dinner is over."

Allison talked a few more minutes, then she handed the phone back to Ammon. She enjoyed hearing his laughter, knowing her parents were teasing him.

The anesthetic began to wear off, and the nurse said they would wait a while to inject more medication so the labor would progress more quickly. As Allison began to feel a degree of pain, she marveled that any woman could do this in a stable.

The pain became more intense as the end drew closer. They finally gave her more medication, and it began to take effect as she was prepared for delivery. A nurse came in and said, "I think your whole family is waiting out in the hall."

"Really?" Ammon said.

"They're not wearing pajamas, are they?" Allison asked, grateful to feel the pain subsiding.

Allison's focus became completely centered on getting this child into the world. She tried to do everything she was told, while Ammon held her hands, coaching and encouraging her. Fearing she would collapse from exhaustion, she put everything she had left into bearing down. She held her breath as the little dark head appeared, and a moment later, the doctor held the bawling infant up for her to see. She laughed and cried and clung to Ammon, vaguely aware that he was doing the same.

"Oh, he's beautiful," Allison murmured. Her hands trembled as she held her new son. How could she not think of Mary? Ammon had been right. This was the ideal way to spend Christmas Eve.

A few minutes later, Ammon's family, including Lupe, huddled in the birthing room, admiring the new addition to the family. Fresh tears came to Allison's eyes as Ammon laid his son in his grandmother's arms. Tears streamed down Lupe's face. Ammon put an arm around Lupe and kissed her brow.

"There's nothing like a newborn child," Lupe said, her voice trembling with age. "It reminds us that life is always starting over, and no matter how we struggle, there is always something good to be found."

"I couldn't have said it better myself, Nana," Ammon said.

Allison took her husband's hand into hers, whispering the words she had heard him say many times last year as she had struggled to come to terms with her own difficulties. "That's what Christmas is all about."

Photo by Nathan Barney

About the Author

Anita Stansfield is an imaginative and prolific writer whose stories of love and romance have captivated the LDS market. *Home for Christmas* is her seventh novel to be published by Covenant; her other best-selling titles include *First Love and Forever* (winner of the 1994-95 Best Fiction Award from the Independent LDS Booksellers), *First Love, Second Chances, Now and Forever, By Love and Grace, A Promise of Forever,* and *Return to Love.*

Anita has been writing since she was in high school, and her work has appeared in *Cosmopolitan* and other publications. She is an active member of the League of Utah Writers.

Anita and her husband, Vince, live with their four children and a cat named "Ivan the Terrible" in Alpine, Utah.